My Dear Boy

EST. 75 1938
YEARS
THE UNIVERSITY OF GEORGIA PRESS 2013

Portrait of Carolyn Clark—Caroline Langston Hughes Clark. Printed by permission of Harold Ober Associates Incorporated. Copyright © 2013 by the Estate of Langston Hughes. Yale Collection of American Literature, Beinecke Rare Book and Manuscript Library.

My Dear Boy

CARRIE HUGHES'S

LETTERS TO

LANGSTON HUGHES,

1926–1938

Edited by
Carmaletta M. Williams
and John Edgar Tidwell

THE UNIVERSITY OF GEORGIA PRESS
Athens & London

The letters written by Carrie Hughes are printed by permission of Harold Ober
Associates Incorporated. Copyright © 2013 by the Estate of Langston Hughes.

© 2013 by the University of Georgia Press
Athens, Georgia 30602
www.ugapress.org
All rights reserved
Set in 11.5/15 Adobe Garamond Pro
Printed and bound by Thomson-Shore

The paper in this book meets the guidelines for
permanence and durability of the Committee on
Production Guidelines for Book Longevity of the
Council on Library Resources.

Printed in the United States of America

17 16 15 14 13 C 5 4 3 2 1

Library of Congress Cataloging-in-Publication Data
Hughes, Carrie, –1938.
  [Correspondence. Selections]
  My dear boy : Carrie Hughes's letters to Langston Hughes, 1926–1938 / edited by
Carmaletta M. Williams and John Edgar Tidwell.
    pages cm
  Includes bibliographical references and index.
    ISBN-13: 978-0-8203-4565-9 (hardcover : alk. paper)
    ISBN-10: 0-8203-4565-2 (hardcover : alk. paper)
  1. Hughes, Carrie, –1938—Correspondence. 2. Hughes, Langston, 1902–1967—
Correspondence. 3. Mothers of authors—United States—Correspondence.
4. African American mothers—Biography. 5. African American authors—Family
relationships. I. Williams, Carmaletta M., [birth]– editor. II. Tidwell, John Edgar,
editor. III. Title. IV. Title: Carrie Hughes's letters to Langston Hughes, 1926–1938.
  PS3515.U274Z48 2013
  818'.5209—dc23

                              2013003511

British Library Cataloging-in-Publication Data available

THIS BOOK IS DEDICATED TO

Our Dear Mothers
> The Late Doris Rebecca Grant
> The Late Verlean L. Tidwell

AND

Our Dear Boys
> Dwight "Chief" Williams
> Jason John Williams
> Nicholas A. Elias
> Levert Tidwell

CONTENTS

FOLLOWING LANGSTON
A Foreword

Late summer 1967. Sumter, South Carolina. *Jet* magazine has just arrived as it does each and every month. Mama sits in her chair reading through the current Black history news, holding the tiny *Jet* pages by their corners and reading aloud in her most operatic voice. She includes in her reading news of any deaths she believes should matter to us children, whether we recognize the names called out or not. She wants us to know that both things and people come and go. Mama and Daddy are lifetime members of the NAACP. They believe in supporting Black cultural institutions. They treat Black publications like modern-day North Stars. *Jet, Ebony, The Crisis* all arrive and take their proper place on the main coffee table like Black constellations—shining up at us. Until we can read for ourselves, we are read to every day of our young lives. I learn very early that there are Black people who must never be forgotten.

James Mercer Langston Hughes died when I was ten years old. The facts were surely read aloud: *Joplin. Grandmother. Kansas. Class Poet. Dream. Harlem. Jazz. Race Pride.* Mama called him a "poet of note," reminding me that I had recited some of his poetry once, "A Dream Deferred" and "The Negro Speaks of Rivers," at Emmanuel Methodist Church for Black History Month. I do not remember this moment as much as I have been reminded of this moment.

Langston Hughes followed me around like a great light. In my neighborhood Langston Hughes was called some variation of the Poet Laureate of the Negro Race. For me—he was exactly that. As a young Black girl of the segregated, then begrudgingly integrated South, he might as well have been the first poet of the whole wide world.

In seventh grade, I started keeping a journal and writing poetry. It would be several years before I would read somewhere, and marvel, that Langston Hughes had been the class poet of his own eighth grade. *The Crisis* magazine that kept arriving long after Hughes was dead was one of the places I began to check the pages of—looking for more from Langston Hughes's many worlds: essays, librettos, plays, autobiography, children's books, jazz histories, solo poems especially. Long after Langston had gone there were other things that kept him alive in me: reading *The Big Sea* and "The Negro Artist and the Racial Mountain" in college, finding *Fire!!* in the Schomburg stacks one summer between graduate school sessions. I followed the life and work of Langston Hughes from discovery to study. I never knew quite where his bright words might lead me. I just knew I had to walk strong into the light.

I was a curiously sensitive, indeed sometimes melancholy Black girl living in the Civil Rights South. I *belonged* to the wide wicked world of the South yet I wanted to know more than anyone seemed to want to tell me. I listened to Daddy's jazz records and wanted more. I listened to Mama read about the Black world out and beyond and wanted to know more. I had questions about the physics of life: Who got to move through the world with their head up all effortless and easy? Who had perfected the act of walking while bowed and bent and looking down? Who got to etch their initials into things like silver cups and write letters on cotton paper made with silk thread? Who wrote and hid their stories on paper bags and napkins? Who only had time to wash and wax? Who had to move on through the world with a sack of sorrow on their shoulders? Who got to dance and be the movie star? Who always died younger with the expected broken heart?

During my search for how to become the poet that I didn't know how to become, the poetry and life of Langston Hughes guided me from all four directions of the universe. I found in James Langston Hughes's life a horizon line, a clear path—stepping stones to get from here to there. Here was a poet born and raised in another small town in America—just like me, from a politically charged family—just like me. A poet raised primarily by his grandmother, who had instilled in him an everlasting sense of race pride—just like me. Here was a poet who had found velocity in books and paper, who had been the class poet at a young age, who wrote dutifully and prolifically from that childhood forward, a poet who had found his way to a historically Black college, who kept honing his Afrocentric landscapes and portraits. Hughes was a poet who jumped freighters and wrote about laziness and labor, who left home and couldn't always be what his mama or his daddy or his people wished, but nevertheless wrote proudly all the way to the end, as a Negro artist. All along the way Langston Hughes picked up and moved mountains around—inside one little Black girl born in the segregated, now integrated South, who held pencils as close as if they were candy canes. Langston Hughes was a blazing light in my wilderness.

Hughes's deep love of his own Blackness, in a world that suggested he be less Black or more anything else, situated me. Langston Hughes's deep love for his Blackness and his primal dedication to say the hard thing with great visual verve, unmasked the persnickety literary world with its constant and great warnings about color lines and political stop signs. Langston Hughes was unbowed. He wrote tirelessly about his affection for Black people. Black people were his study and his course in life. Through the prism of his pen, Langston Hughes taught me that Blackness held everything under the sun.

No poet can follow Langston Hughes, but, of course, many have come after. I count myself in that number. We poets-after-Hughes keep scribbling out here in the "big sea," hoping to give honor to our own, as well as to our great poet of note, who set so many of us sailing.

Nikky Finney
Lexington, Kentucky
November 10, 2012

PREFACE

October 29, 1928

I want you to help me this time and I won't bother you ever again. Dear, why don't you love me. Why aren't we more loving and chummy. Why don't you ever confide in me. I know I have no sense to help you in your work but I'd enjoy your confidence. Now Langston, I have no one else to talk to, you will agree with me and help me won't you if you can? Please don't be angry because I want to go, for I'd see everyone I ever knew so I am wild to go.

February 15, 1933

Yes, your mother is an actress at last, the dream I dreamed as a little child is very near realized. I am one of the principals in Hall Johnson's show "Run Little Chillun Run."

February 3, 1938

"I get out very little and am nearly crazy being so lonely, sometimes. But I can't stand it. Car fare is so high one can't go often now days. I have 6 months."

These epigraphs are snapshots framing the fascinating, albeit conflicted life of Carolyn "Carrie" Hughes Clark—mother of the renowned poet, fiction writer, playwright, and essayist Langston Hughes. Between 1926 and 1930, when Langston is in his twenties, she worries, cajoles, demands, and generally holds her son emotionally hostage. During the next few years, she flies high, feeling free and valued as a person, an artist, and a woman as she realizes her lifelong dream of performing onstage to an audience of adoring fans. Toward the end of the 1930s, she spirals downward into a lonely abyss of bad health, isolation, poverty, and death. When she writes her dutiful son in February 1938 about her sense of devastation and loneliness, she did not have six months to live—only four. She died June 3 in New York City, where her "dear boy" had taken her for care in the time she had remaining.

My Dear Boy focuses on an important but heretofore largely unexplored dimension of Langston Hughes. What is known about Langston has been nicely captured in a number of well-argued biographies and collections of his correspondence. A perfect complement to them, however, is available in the underused collection of extant correspondence written by his mother. Her letters are a treasure trove of ideas and information that shed new light on Langston, especially his family dynamic and aesthetic achievement. The perspective on their relationship that emerges from Carrie's letters to her dear son is often one of insensitivity, if not downright pain. But eliciting sympathy for traumatic family interactions is *not* the purpose of this book. The goal instead is to explicate Hughes family dynamics. Carrie's role in orchestrating the interrelationships of family members is crucial to understanding their effect on Langston, including his response to her many entreaties and how he embeds familial themes in the art he creates in the mid-1920s to the late 1930s—the period during which she corresponds with him. Her letters, then, force her out of the shadows and into the same light of those who have already been considered significant influences on his aesthetic development.

The letters in this book, which cover twelve years, 1926–38, are found in the Langston Hughes Papers in the James Weldon Johnson Collection at Yale University's Beinecke Library. Why Carrie's letters have received virtually no attention en masse is difficult to determine. One explanation may entail availability. Precisely when her letters were added to her son's voluminous archive at the Beinecke Library is uncertain. Prior to his death in 1967, Langston had been shipping boxes of his papers to the collection for nearly twenty years, and a large group was sent soon after his death. It is safe to assume that Carrie's letters were for a longtime simply included in his enormous body of papers with no special effort to identify or isolate them. Sadly, a record of who had access to the manuscripts and letters is lost to history too. Shifting library policies meant that some materials were made public as they were catalogued and processed, while others remained restricted for various reasons.

Scholars have long acknowledged Carrie in their work on Langston, some even using fugitive letters as evidence for their arguments. Regennia N. Williams and Carmaletta M. Williams quoted from some of them in their coauthored essay "Mother to Son: The Letters from Carrie Hughes Clark to Langston Hughes." With that exception, however, no one has probed her collected letters for their own integrity or the significance they hold for Langston's aesthetic development and output. *My Dear Boy* undertakes such an interrogation.

While editing this body of correspondence, we were presented with a number of challenges. For instance, although Carrie Hughes was an extremely bright woman, she wrote with little or no regard for posterity or publication. Thus she often expressed herself quite informally and gave little attention to issues of complete sentences as well as proper punctuation, spelling, and grammar. For the most part, we resisted the urge to "fix" them: the letters are published as written. In a few cases, however, we felt the need to facilitate readability and clarity. Here we made silent emendations, such as adding periods or dropped characters, to make the reading smoother.

The letters present further complications. Carrie often wrote across the top, down the sides, and on the backs of pages. A few of the letters continue on after the closing "Lovingly yours, Mamma," while others begin before the salutation, typically "My Dear Boy." When appropriate, we place these "side notes" at the end when they read like postscripts, or before the salutation when they appear there. In each instance, we attempted to preserve the letter's integrity by keeping sentences in the order of their creation.

We also found it important to preserve Carrie's exact wording and spelling because they more clearly demonstrate her moods, voice, and eventually the deterioration in her skills and her health. Where her handwriting became especially shaky, we have provided notes to explain the thoughts she attempted to communicate. To Carrie's habit of double- or triple-underlining words, we have used brackets indicating this practice as her mode of emphasis.

Authoritatively documenting the dates of the letters was another problem. Many of them were either entirely undated or labeled with a month, date, or day of the week but no year. We placed these letters chronologically by making the best determination we could about the sequence of events in Carrie's and Langston's lives. We also used place of residence to make decisions regarding chronological order, aided by names of cities and states included in the letters. Not all names of people and places will be familiar to today's readers, so we have used notes to explain ones we were able to identify.

A further word about names: some biographers and critics strenuously argue that referring to subjects by their first name is akin to claiming an undue personal acquaintanceship or intimate familial knowledge. Arguments rooted in gender perspectives liken this practice, politically, to erasing a woman's identity and thus her complexity. In opting for the more familiar names of "Carrie" and "Langston," we claim no special relationship with this mother and her son. We are very much aware that self-identification can engender complexities, such as those that derive from Carrie's naming and renaming of herself. We believe, however, that the brevity of first names intensifies the conflicted familial cohesion and entanglement *My Dear Boy* explores.

Structurally, this book eschews the traditional introduction and conclusion for a more integrative pattern we designate "prologue" and "epilogue." These echo here an appropriate device in African American rhetorical and musical traditions: call and response. The prologue (the call) introduces Carrie and our method for reading her correspondence, while the epilogue (the response) registers Langston's answers to his mother by examining his creative writing. Together, prologue and epilogue frame the letters and the headnotes that preface each section. Our intent is that this arrangement will provide a nearly cohesive narrative.

Our decision to forgo the point-counterpoint of Carrie and Langston exchanging letters was born out of necessity. Langston's letters, unlike his mother's, are still widely dispersed in libraries and personal collections, and there is no systematic listing of them. Furthermore, Carrie repeatedly begged Langston to write back to her, which tells us that he did not routinely respond to every letter she sent him. When Langston did write her back, his few extant letters are emotionally unrevealing, in keeping with his well-known predisposition for creating a wall around his innermost feelings. One only has to consult Charles Nichols's and Emily Bernard's collections of Langston's correspondence to bear out this propensity. As a way of divining his views on familial relationships, we turned to his most typical mode of expression: his art.

In the absence of a full-scale biography of Carrie Hughes, then, we hope this book will provide a useful portrait of her life as well as a context in which to view it.

ABBREVIATIONS

ARI   Rampersad, Arnold. *The Life of Langston Hughes, Volume I: 1902–1941. I, Too, Sing America.* New York: Oxford University Press, 1986.

ARII   Rampersad, Arnold. *The Life of Langston Hughes, Volume II: 1941–1967. I Dream A World.* New York: Oxford University Press, 1988.

CVV   Bernard, Emily, ed. *Remember Me to Harlem: The Letters of Langston Hughes and Carl Van Vechten.* New York: Random House, 2002.

LHP   Langston Hughes Papers, James Weldon Johnson Collection, Beinecke Rare Book and Manuscript Library, Yale University.

WW   Hughes, Langston. *I Wonder as I Wander.* New York: Hill and Wang. 1956.

CHRONOLOGY

1869 Charles Langston and Mary Leary wed on January 18. Charles brings a foster son, Desalines, to the marriage, and Mary brings Loise, her daughter with Lewis Sheridan Leary. (Leary died from injuries incurred during the 1859 raid on the federal arsenal at Harper's Ferry with John Brown.)

1870 A son, Nathaniel Turner Langston, is born to Charles and Mary.

1873 Carolina Mercer Langston is born on February 22 to Charles and Mary Langston on a farm five miles north of Lawrence, Kansas, near Lakeview.

1888 Charles Langston moves his family to Lawrence in order to manage his part interest in a thriving grocery store on Massachusetts Street, a main thoroughfare in town.

      Carrie is "the Belle of Black Lawrence" in her social life.

1891 Charles Langston founds the Inter-State Literary Society. Carrie reads before the club and becomes a star in the Progressive Club of St. Luke A.M.E. Church.

1892 Charles Langston dies in Lawrence, Kansas, in November.

1893 Carrie graduates from Lawrence High School and works as "Deputy District Clerk" in the Lawrence City Hall.

1894   Under the name "Mercer Langston," Carrie completes a ten-week course in kindergarten and primary school education in April at Kansas State Normal School in Emporia.

1897   Brother Nathaniel Turner Langston is killed in a workplace accident at the local flour mill.

1898   Carrie arrives in Guthrie, Oklahoma Territory, located twelve miles from the all-Black town of Langston, named for her famous uncle. She meets James Nathaniel Hughes there.

1899   Carrie and James marry on April 30 in Guthrie. The couple moves to Joplin, Missouri, where he works as a stenographer for the Lincoln Mining Company.

1900   Carrie and James report to a census taker the loss of a son "Hughs Inf of JM (col)," who appears to have been buried "beneath the gravel" of Joplin's potter's field, in Fairview Cemetery, on February 8.

1901   Carrie joins James in Buffalo, New York, in the early spring.

        Near September 1, Carrie is in St. Louis with James's youngest brother, John.

1902   Langston Hughes is born near midnight on February 1, in Joplin.

1903   James works as confidential secretary for the Pullman Company in Mexico City. He is admitted to the bar in Mexico. Carrie takes Langston to her mother in Lawrence, thus inaugurating a pattern of abandoning and reuniting with him.

1907   The separated couple attempts to reconcile April 14 in Mexico, where James has taken up residence. An earthquake aborts this effort. Carrie returns to the United States, leaves Langston with his grandmother, and takes off for Topeka.

1908   Langston lives with Carrie in Topeka and attends Harrison, a predominately White elementary school.

1909 Carrie returns Langston to her mother in Lawrence in April. Carrie moves to Colorado Springs, Colorado.

1910 Mary Leary Langston takes her grandson to Osawatomie, Kansas, where former president Theodore Roosevelt honors her first husband's sacrifice at Harper's Ferry. This follows the commemoration she received in 1859, when a friend presented her with the bullet-riddled, bloodstained shawl he wore at his death.

1913 Gwyn Shannon "Kit" Clark, the son of Carrie's second husband, Homer, is born on September 24.

1915 Mary Langston dies on April 8. By then Carrie has divorced James and married Homer Clark, who brings his two-year-old son to the family. Carrie leaves Langston with family friends, "Uncle" James W. Reed and "Auntie" Mary Reed. Late summer he joins Carrie and family in Lincoln, Illinois, where he is one of two Black children in the school. He is in the eighth grade.

 At the end of summer the family joins Homer in Cleveland, Ohio.

1917 Homer leaves for a job in Chicago, and Carrie joins him. Langston lives alone in an attic apartment in Cleveland.

1918 Langston visits Carrie and Gwyn in Chicago over the summer. Homer moves on. By the end of summer Langston has saved "a little money" and returns alone to Cleveland to finish high school.

1919 Carrie and Gwyn join Langston in Cleveland. In June Langston travels with his father to Mexico, but he returns in September.

1920 Langston graduates from high school. A month later he returns to Mexico and stays a year. He sends money to Carrie from his earnings teaching English.

1921 Carrie and Gwyn move to a small one-room apartment in New York City. She convinces Langston to move in with them. In September, he enrolls at Columbia University and moves into a dormitory.

1922   Carrie, Homer, and Gwyn live in McKeesport, Pennsylvania.

Langston lives in a rooming house in Harlem at 156 West 141st Street and works on a ship literally going nowhere—it is moored in the Hudson River.

1923   Langston boards the freighter *West Hesseltine* in Manhattan on June 23, throws all his books overboard (except for Walt Whitman's *Leaves of Grass*), and works his way to Africa. In October returns to Carrie in McKeesport with a monkey and less than a dollar. A furious Carrie sells the monkey. On Christmas Eve Langston is at work on another ship, which docks in Rotterdam.

1924   Langston meets Arna Bontemps who remains Hughes's closest friend for life. James Hughes marries his housekeeper, Frau Schulz, in January. Langston sails out to sea on February 5 after not hearing from Alain Locke about admission and scholarship to Howard University. Langston deserts the *McKeesport* in Holland, purchases a visa to France, and lives in Paris. He returns to New York in November. Soon after, he moves to Washington, D.C., to live with Carrie and relatives.

1925   At Christmas, Langston receives notice of scholarship to attend Lincoln University in Pennsylvania.

1926   February 14, Langston leaves a furious Carrie, who is living with Gwyn in Atlantic City, New Jersey, to attend Lincoln University, where "neither crime nor bad grammar" were tolerated. He spends summer in Harlem rooming house and contributes to the only issue of *Fire!!*, which critics pan.

1927   Langston meets patron Charlotte Osgood Mason. She offers him $150 a month for the first year to free him for "artistic flight."

1928   Mrs. Mason arranges for Gwyn to board and attend school in Springfield, Massachusetts. Carrie sabotages the arrangement because she is "too lonely" without him.

Langston stores the Harper's Ferry shawl in a safe deposit box in a Fifth Avenue bank.

1929   Langston and Mrs. Mason clash over what she perceives as ingratitude. Langston has Thanksgiving dinner with Carrie, Homer, and Gwyn in Atlantic City.

1930   Langston is in Cuba on February 25.

1931   "Scottsboro Boys" arrested on March 25. Langston sympathizes with their cause.

         Langston lives with Carrie in Cleveland for three months, leaving on April 1.

         Langston moves to a Harlem YMCA upon returning from Haiti.

1932   Carrie and Langston visit Lawrence and stay with "Auntie"—now Mary Reed Campbell—in mid-March. Carrie continues to live in Cleveland, but Langston sails for Russia on June 14 to help make a movie titled *Black and White*. The production is never completed, but he remains there for a year.

1933   Carrie appears in Hall Johnson's production *Run, Little Chillun*.

1934   On October 22, James Nathaniel Hughes dies in Mexico of complications from several strokes. Neither Langston nor Carrie is mentioned in his will.

1935   In a May 14 letter, Carrie writes Langston that she has a "very bad blood tumor" on her breast. Langston lives in Mexico. On October 24, *Mulatto* begins a two-year run on Broadway.

1938   Carrie dies of breast cancer on June 3.

My Dear Boy

PROLOGUE

The renowned poet, fiction writer, playwright, essayist, and humorist Langston Hughes has been the subject of countless biographies, critical studies, celebratory conferences and symposia, and other well-earned acknowledgments of his enduring body of creative writing. Hughes is widely acclaimed for his shaping influence on the development of African American literature and for his generous assistance to a younger generation of writers emerging in the early 1960s. For all the careful scrutiny given to this luminary, it is curious that one of his biggest influences has gone virtually unexamined: his mother, Carolyn "Carrie" Hughes Clark. In nearly all the attention devoted to Hughes's blues and jazz ethos, humor, vernacular voicings, and poetic innovations, the possible role Carrie may have played in her son's vast array of stylistic experiments and literary production has been nearly ignored.

Conceptually, the matter of "influence" remains a conflicted notion. However, the idea we propose has little to do with establishing *literary* precursors, demonstrating convergence with or divergence from the work of other poets and fiction writers, or employing other such relational strategies with regard to authors and book reading.[1] Fundamentally, *My Dear Boy* sets forth "influence," using the correspondence Carrie sent to Langston, as a means of extrapolating a subtle familial transaction revealed in such representative works as his *Not without Laughter*, *Mulatto*, "Negro Mother," and *Soul Gone Home*. Our use of letters to place the Self in perspective falls within a well-explored tradition.

In her impressive study *The Cultural Work of the Late Nineteenth-Century Hostess*, Susan K. Harris thoughtfully contextualizes an important perspective on the letter-writing tradition. She begins with the most common assumption about personal letters as a rhetorical act: that "they are private conversations between individuals" (51). Using William Decker's *Epistolary Practices*, she complicates this idea by noting that most letters have "multiple interfaces." She continues: "Decker's postmodern term 'interface' . . . helps us to think of letters as a two-way process instead of as a purely unidirectional, inscriber-to-recipient, mode of writing. . . . [T]hinking in terms of multiple interfaces enables us to consider the effect of the letter on the person writing it as well as the person or persons receiving it" (52). In his own way, Faulkner scholar James G. Watson offers an insight similar to Harris's: "Personal letters are fragments of autobiography in which the Self and the Word are designedly one. They deliver the letter writer figuratively into the hands of the reader, but because they do, the Self written in private letters is vulnerable to intrusions" (*William* xii). Implicit in Watson's astute observation are two key points. First, in Faulkner's letters, the relationship between Self and Word is a self-conscious, deliberate working out of personality and self-expression. Thus the art of letter writing becomes for Faulkner a rehearsal for his fiction. Second, while the private nature of his correspondence is not intended for posterity or to be widely shared, the letters are nevertheless open to the interpretations others might bring to them.

Although Carrie's letters, even to the most casual reader, are not intended to reveal the reading communities Harris discusses, it is possible to extrapolate "multiple interfaces." They are without the epistolary conventions governing Faulkner's public and private correspondence, but her letters are nevertheless open to interpretation. She obviously did not write with posterity in mind. No doubt she would rankle at the examination of her correspondence for what it divulges about her own person and her contentious familial relationships. Such an exploration, though, serves a higher purpose than merely "airing dirty laundry" or exposing an idiosyncratic personality. The transaction between Self and Word in her letters manifests an inextricably linked emotional connection between her desperate pleas to Langston and his aesthetic response to her demanding entreaties. Thus the "interface" in her letters is a two-way process between writer and recipient: there is communication with Langston and a revelation of deep insight into her Self. Using the analysis we propose reveals a vulnerability that public readers might readily perceive.

As this prologue demonstrates, Carrie's letters reveal a life fraught with a complexity and complication heretofore unexplored and with a depth that offers her life as a shaping influence on Langston's art. The epilogue frames his response to the intricacies of her life, especially in the 1920s and 1930s. By inscribing their relationship as a series of familial conflicts, Langston confronts their family ties *indirectly*, via aesthetics. Between this "call" and "response" lies a body of Carrie's letters, letters that function as epistolary testaments, placing a mother's relationship to her well-known writer son in a wholly new perspective.

A fuller appreciation of her letters first requires an assessment of the image of Carrie that comes to light in critical discussions about her. Biographers and historians generally assert that Carrie as woman, wife, and mother fails to be doting, kind, loving, nurturing, or maternal. Instead, she appears in most studies as a complex and "difficult" woman. How do writers reach this conclusion? It can be argued that from her act of self-naming, of projecting a particular representation of herself, emerges a personality that betrays eccentricity and conflict. Born Carolina Mercer Langston, on Saturday, February 22, 1873, in her adult life she successively or alternately referred to herself as "Caroline Langston," "Carolyn Hughes" (after her marriage to James N. Hughes, Langston's father), "Carolyn Hughes Clark" (after her divorce from James Hughes and marriage to Homer Clark), and "Carrie Clark." She also spelled Clark with and without a final "e." Despite what may seem inconsiderate decisions, arbitrary choices, or simple necessity, Carrie, wittingly or not, participates in the power of naming to define her sense of self. As she seeks to project the image of a strong, fiercely independent woman, however, she invariably contradicts this representation by using emotional appeals, evoking guilt, expressing anger, or simply importuning to coerce her son's love, affection, and especially his financial support. Therein lies the source of her enigmatic personality, which more deeply probing scholars, such as Arnold Rampersad and Faith Berry, uncover as they seek awareness of who she was and where she fit into Langston's life.

Typically, however, Carrie appears in most Hughes scholarship as a brief citation, an obligatory nod to the fact that she gave birth to him. Other discussions either reiterate a few facts about her birth into a socially and politically prominent family or reveal personality traits and quirks that imply an indelible mark on Hughes's own struggles to define himself and his art. In her teenage years, Carrie enjoyed a rather privileged social position. She lived as a legatee of a prominent ancestral past. This is not to suggest that she merely basked in the glow of an abundant, glorious family history. She was aware of what critic Charles H. Nichols, in another context, describes as an inheritance of "austerity and dedicated moral purpose." In part, this means that with parents barely one generation removed from the postbellum imperative of racial uplift, she too "felt the obligation to prove that Africans were not only educable but capable of high culture" (Nichols 6). The racial imperative she embraces manifested itself in "her taste for musicals, plays, [and] novels" as well as in her practice of elocution and longing for the professional stage (ARI 9). Her racial raison d'être did not end there. Arnold Rampersad elaborates: "Carrie Langston had become at fifteen one of the belles of Black Lawrence, Kansas. At eighteen, encouraged by her father, she read papers before his Inter-State Literary Society and even recited her own poems. Light olive in complexion, stylish and popular, Carrie became a star in the St. Luke's Progressive Club. When the rival Warren Street Second Baptist Church founded its own cultural society, she was elected 'Critic'" (ARI 9).

To characterize Carrie's manifestation of the ancestral imperative as largely artistic is not to deny her awareness of the family's political heritage. She understood that her father, Charles Langston, had been a passionate abolitionist, an ardent supporter of John Brown, and a prominent figure in Kansas Republican politics. As president of the Colored Benevolent Society, grandmaster of the Black Masonic Fraternity, and associate editor of a local Black newspaper, the *Historic Times*, he served at the heart of Lawrence's social activities. She knew quite well the history of other fam-

ily members. John Mercer Langston, her uncle, had taken degrees from
Oberlin College, received admission to the Ohio bar, become a professor
of law and acting president at Howard University, and served in the U.S.
Congress as a representative from Virginia. Her mother, Mary, an abolitionist, was a widow before marrying the man who would become Carrie's
father. Mary's first husband, Lewis Sheridan Leary, had died from wounds
suffered during the attack on the Harper's Ferry arsenal with John Brown.
Ten years later she would marry Charles Langston. Carrie embraced this
storied past and saw herself as part of it.

Her heart, though, was fixed on stage performance. Being Black, a
woman, and a Black woman with marginal talent posed handicaps that
Carrie could not easily surmount. In 1892, her world was shattered when
her father died. The family had enjoyed prominence, but his death left
them impoverished. Her life then became paradoxical. While she aspired
to a future in the limelight of onstage performance, economic necessity
forced her into more prosaic labor. She managed employment as school-
teacher, stenographer, and domestic before a series of local stage roles finally led to her dream of appearing on Broadway, in Hall Johnson's 1933
folk drama *Run, Little Chillun*. Along the way, constant poverty would
foster a struggle, and she persistently pursued the rainbow's end from the
midst of the storm.

Thus Carrie's passionate pursuit of her dreams of a successful stage career ran counter to the reality of the world in which she was forced to
live. As generally represented in the scholarship on Langston, she emerges
as a self-centered, demanding, needy, and frustrated woman. Rowena Jelliffe of Cleveland's Karamu Players recalled, in an interview with Arnold
Rampersad, that Carrie, in certain ways, "had become a hard woman. . . .
She was concerned only with money. She was always pounding Langston
about it. Carrie hammered at him all the time with the idea that he wasn't
going the way she wanted him to go. She thought he was wasting his time
writing poetry" (ARI 38–39). From this description emerges not just her
conflicted relationship with Langston but also the guilt and depression
engendered in him. Hughes's admission of hatred for his father is well
known, but the resentment he felt for his mother is not as explicitly stated.

No doubt these feelings were exacerbated by what scholars point to as her restive spirit, a "pattern of constant movement" as critic Onwuchekwa Jemie calls it (xxv). Her peripatetic nature culminated in an often physical but also emotional distance from her son. Shortly after Langston's 1902 birth, Carrie moved with him from Joplin, Missouri, to her mother's home in Lawrence. By biographer Faith Berry's account, this relocation inaugurated a life in which Langston lived in seven cities before he was twelve years old (Berry, *Langston* 4). An easy conclusion is that she was simply incapable of providing Langston with a stable home, but this conclusion is too hastily derived. Carrie's rootlessness and detachment meant that she was able to maintain only a tenuous connection with him at best. The long times they spent apart and the tension between them when they were together were not conducive to developing a cohesive relationship.

The uncertainties of Carrie's life, caused in part by the economic unpredictability of the Depression, forced her to be "dependent upon him, [even though she was] not attentive" (Berry, *Langston* 11). Carrie suffered the on-and-off attention of her second husband, Homer Clark, whose own wanderlust kept him constantly searching new towns for employment. He left his own son, Gwyn (nicknamed "Kit"), in Carrie's care, thus increasing the pressure on her for the family's economic survival. Carrie seemed unaware that Langston's enormous literary reputation did not translate into financial success. She persistently approached him for money, as if his coffers were always filled. Her requests evolved into demands, as when, in his senior year of high school, she engaged him in a tug of war between school and work (Berry, *Langston* 21). For Carrie, Langston's potential as a laborer and contributor to her financial well-being was infinitely more valuable than his education. Gone was her sense of rich family history in which education was fundamental to the family's success. She needed him to be a source of income so that her life and leisure would be provided for.

Until her death in 1938, her pattern of "importuning and flightiness" caused Langston no small amount of hardship (ARI 305). Understandably, he felt trapped. On one hand, his father tempted him with promises of money, which, like the thirty pieces of silver, would require him to embrace self-hatred and racial hatred. On the other, Carrie reminded her dutiful son of his obligation to care for her. She desired and expected Langston to shower her with financial support and attention. Rejecting his father was easier for him, as he did when withdrawing from the School of Mines program at Columbia University. However, while "Hughes loved his mother," as Rampersad wrote, "a true reconciliation with her was impossible; his childhood loneliness made him suspicious of her and of all women. Except perhaps one" (ARI 167). As discussed shortly, Langston's relationship with Carrie sent him looking for a surrogate mother—which he would find in Charlotte Osgood Mason.

Carrie's letters, therefore, function as a gateway into understanding a number of issues that derive from a complex familial relationship. They direct us to a deeper understanding and fuller appreciation of Carrie as a person, a woman, and a mother—a representation greater than the one Hughes biographers typically capture. Her correspondence clearly delineates the strained, distant, and incongruous relationship she has with her son, thus documenting the barriers to developing a close familial alliance. As testaments of a nonfunctioning family, her letters, we argue, provide the source material that Hughes transforms into meaningful art. To understand how these complicated family relations become "influences," it is necessary to employ a theoretical construct that unravels the complex nature of the family relations shaping his work.

Bowen Family Systems Theory

Arnold Rampersad first called for a biographical approach to Black subjects that made greater use of psychological theories in *Afro-American Literary Study in the 1990s*. At the same time, he provided an admirable response to his own call in an exhaustive two-volume history of Langston's life. Even though his method is a subtle immersion into Freudian psychoanalytic theories, Rampersad largely explores the individual Self to the exclusion of other nurturing or natural influences, leading to what Jerome Bump, in quoting Foucault, concludes is "'a socially isolated and individualistic view of the self' that 'precludes the possibility of enduring attachments or responsibilities to another'" (328). Scholars interested in applying psychological theory to literary analysis often point to the weakness in the theory of the Oedipal Complex, one of Freud's central tenets, as evincing a need for a more inclusive psychological approach. Generally, there is some agreement with Storhoff, who writes: "The Oedipal Complex as a theoretical orientation . . . oversimplifies because it does *not* address the self-in-family" (291). Framing Carrie within the *family unit* and not just as the image of a neglectful, self-aggrandizing, insensitive mother has interpretive advantages. This larger context enables a broader portrait, one that explores causal relationships in her interactions with others.

The most appropriate heuristic for this approach is psychiatrist Murray Bowen's Family Systems Theory (FST) because it provides a valuable means for interrogating the "multiple interfaces" of Carrie's letters and their significance for the aesthetic vision driving Langston from the mid-1920s to the late 1930s. FST gets at Carrie's motivations and the role familial relationships play in developing them. Thus the focus shifts from the individual to the family and the processes by which the members interact with one another. Simply put, an examination of "inter-relational processes" investigates with greater scrutiny the evidence usually gathered to condemn Carrie. Bowen's theory of the family helps to explicate Carrie's complexity as well as Langston's response to it by using three interconnected concepts: self-differentiation, fusion (or enmeshment), and triangulation.

Differentiation

Bowen posits self-differentiation as an ability to adhere to one's own principles, regardless of the degree of emotional pressure one experiences. As implemented by researchers Johnson, Buboltz, and Seemann, Bowen's concept of differentiation of self "refers to an individual's ability to function in an autonomous and self-directed manner without being controlled by family members or significant others and without emotionally cutting oneself off from these significant relationships. . . . In other words, differentiated individuals are able to separate themselves from unresolved emotional attachments in their families without severing significant relationships" (191). Elements foundational to the building of self-differentiation are present at birth. An individual's childhood and adolescent familial relationships determine, however, to what degree that Self will be fully developed—that is, differentiated from others in the family. For example, young children who assert themselves in seemingly willful ways are said to have "minds of their own." They are very much part of the family system and bond with others in the family, but they are developing their own personalities and distinguishing themselves from their siblings, parents, and others. Those children are self-differentiating themselves, placing themselves apart from others in their sphere.

In demonstrating the literary uses of Bowen's theory, Schiff writes compellingly of Philip Roth's novels: "Basically, [differentiation] is the level of one's emotional maturity and individuality. . . . A person with a well differentiated 'self' recognizes his realistic dependence on others, but he can stay calm and clear-headed enough in the face of conflict, criticism, and rejection" (33). In effect, this presents a fight to retain one's own sense of value in the face of efforts to make one conform to values deleterious to one's core beliefs. Individuals with the strength to withstand the push to become like the others are well self-differentiated. The weaker ones, those who capitulate to outside pressure, are poorly self-differentiated.

Such was the task for Carrie. With the deaths of her father (1892) and her brother Nat Turner Langston (1899) as well as the departure from Lawrence of her sister Loise and another brother, Desalines, Carrie was left to contend with a mother who opposed her forays into theater and the arts. From their contest of wills emerged the challenge to Carrie's self-differentiation. To be at least moderately well differentiated, communicate effectively, and function autonomously through times of high stress, both Carrie and her mother had to be capable of controlling their own emotions. Both needed to understand the necessity for a realistic interdependence. Each could have helped the other and both could have retained their individuation. Instead, Carrie essentially abandoned her mother during their time of highest stress to attend college, which in itself is a self-differentiation tactic. At a later stress point, she left Langston in the care of the extremely impoverished Mary. This should have been an opportunity for mother and daughter to fuse appropriately, in a manner that would promote self-differentiation. Carrie's abandonment of Langston, however, forced Mary to fuse with functional kin, James and Mary Reed, for survival.

Fusion (or Enmeshment)

Bowen's premise—that the family is an emotional unit with complex relationships—clearly indicates the small number of families who easily process the concepts that make a strong functioning unit. Few families are able to navigate successfully the inevitable stress and conflicts that accompany life and still remain a cohesive unit with everyone retaining strong, individual personalities. In order to achieve success, members of the family must be able to process a number of factors, including the ability to communicate well with each other; to be well differentiated, which is the ability to develop and emerge from stressful situations strong and independent; to use adequate problem-solving skills; to bond appropriately and develop cohesive relationships especially in times of high stress; and to control affect and emotion. Less successful families find themselves beset with further issues. For example, times of high tension and stress, such as extreme poverty, require additional processes such as emotional fusion, during which the family bands together to help each other. When this is done appropriately, the members emerge from the stress with their individuality intact, thus ensuring the survival of the family. Inappropriate fusion, however, comes at the cost of losing individuation. Fusion, therefore, signifies the extent of parents' over-involvement in each other's life and the lives of their children, which generally leads to the loss of psychological boundaries (Storhoff 303n2).

Families, including the Hughes-Clark family, undergo both predictable and unpredictable changes as they develop. Part of determining such changes means assessing the extent to which family members, whether willing or not, are intensely connected by emotions. For example, the amount of tension in the familial relationship dictates the extent to which family members enjoy or resent the emotional investments necessary to sustain the relationship. Those emotions and that investment are not always comforting or beneficial. Often people feel disconnected from their families. This estrangement is not measured by distance. People sitting next to each other can feel distant. Conversely, family members half a world away can feel emotionally close to each other. Having determined the degree of family connectedness, it is possible to show the importance of emotional survival and the need for individuation.

One of the most important guarantees of the emotional bonding of a connected family is effective communication. However, one of the most prevalent problems in family processes is *ineffective* communication, when family members are incapable of explaining their needs, wants, desires, goals, and ambitions to each other. They lack the ability to articulate or develop appropriate responses. Family members must learn how to solicit and express information in clear, nonthreatening ways. Healthy communication results when they attempt to understand coded language, the language people use to keep safe, and to express themselves directly and clearly. Healthy communication allows family members to learn from and accept each other's individuation and self-differentiation.

During the last two decades of the nineteenth century, Carrie, in her formative years, grew up in what seemed to be the quintessential well-connected, emotionally strong blended family, capable of thriving in spite of the omnipresence of Jim Crow. As previously stated, she had the opportunity to become self-differentiated by asserting herself in her family and in her community, building strong relationships, and developing and maintaining her individuality. The world of this socially engaged, highly popular, beautiful young Black woman of Lawrence was severely tested, however, when her immediate family was decimated by departures, financial ruin, and death. Nevertheless, Carrie conveniently forgets the cohesive family times when she confesses in her letters that she has "never been happy."

Instead of appropriate fusion, Carrie begins a pattern of movement and stasis in which her self-centered demands divide each family system in which she participates. She and James divorce when Langston is very young. Homer leaves her and returns many times until eventually he completely abandons her. As an adult Langston does not want to live with her for any extended time. Only Gwyn, an underage boy with no other familial support during most of the period during which the letters in this book were written, 1926–38, finds a strong family relationship with Carrie. She seems to dote on him, as in this typical letter to Langston: "Gwyn started school today. He came back so tired, he is not strong and eats very little" (September 19, 1932). Her doting is not an indication of love or generosity. Instead, it reveals that the Hughes-Clarks are not a strong, self-differentiated family but an inappropriately fused one. Carrie, who is primarily responsible for the dysfunction, prevents everyone from reaching true individuation. For example, later in 1932, when Carrie and Gwyn are living apart, the stress in her voice shifts from doting to mild concern: "I heard from Gwyn [who] said he was getting on all ok. . . . Homer will go over to [him as] soon as he gets the money. I hope so for Gwyn needs some one with him" (November 14, 1932). This adds to the tension in her relationship with Langston as she never displayed the same concern for her own "dear boy."

Creating a climate in which family members want to support each other unconditionally demands the ability to be rational and respectful of each other. This is especially imperative in situations where a cohesive family unit is necessary for survival. To retain her individuation and allow her son the same, Carrie needed the ability to contain her emotions and retain clear cognition during times of conflict, criticism, rejection, and stress. Instead, she reacts to each life situation on a purely emotional level. Research bears out that emotion and cognition are inseparable. If emotions are out of control, it is extremely difficult to think clearly. None of the members of Carrie's nuclear family, including James, Homer, Langston, and Gwyn, was self-differentiated enough to create a familial balance, overrule her rants, ignore her tirades, work together as a unit, or even help each other.

The more poorly differentiated a person is, the greater the importance of opinions and acceptance by others. The need for the approval and support of others becomes central to the well-being and individuation of less-differentiated members of the same family. Langston's need for Carrie's attention, approval, and support contributes to his being less than fully differentiated. Those hurtful, hateful, longing emotions that abandoned children develop due to ineffective bonding or cohesion within their family systems reinforce the emotional and physical distances between parent and child. Seldom are these distances ever resolved or reconciled. Instead, the child typically becomes the family member who works the hardest to accommodate others in an effort to reduce tension within the family. Langston went past what was comfortable to a place where his health and sustainability were at risk—he sometimes went without food—in an attempt to accommodate Carrie's demands. This tactic rarely works. Instead of being resolved, problems become intensified, unity and teamwork suffer, and anxiety escalates. At that point, connectedness with family becomes more stressful and less comforting. The over-accommodating family member, in this case Langston, suffers most from the strain and usually tries to disconnect.

The view from Carrie's side of this relationship reveals that what appears to be a conscious emotional manipulation of their relationship actually betrays a poorly differentiated self. She often couched her entreaties for money as tests of his love for her. As she begged or demanded money, she simultaneously accused him of not loving her. She insisted that if he really did love her, he would send her money to demonstrate his affections. He usually acceded to her demands, even if he had to borrow the money. In response, Carrie would then fill her letters with loving epithets. She highly praised Langston for loving her so much, sometimes *too* much. In these instances, Carrie unwittingly revealed that the core of her seeming manipulations lay in her being poorly self-differentiated and possibly unaware of the realities of their relationship.

This was especially poignant when she lamented her inability to show her love for him more clearly. In 1929, on his birthday, she wrote: "Mother's love and prayers are for many happy returns of this day, for her only darling son. For in spite of all, you are mine and I do faithfully love you and dearly, passionately love you *even if I can't show it to you*" (emphasis added). These emotional pleadings sound manipulative when they are followed by her standard mantra rooted in her poverty: "being poor is absolutely an irrevocable fact so can't help you any at all." The fact that Carrie saw poverty as "irrevocable" strengthened her emotional fusion with

Langston and pushed her further from being self-differentiated. Indeed, it added to the hopelessness she felt in her ability to change her life for the better.

The more Carrie vacillated between efforts to express deep loving maternal feelings for her son and withholding them, the more intense the friction between mother and son. Langston worked extremely hard in the hope that she would make good on her promises of love. He then recoiled in the wake of the frequent venomous tirades. He no doubt found her acts of withdrawal confusing and hurtful. Her rants effectively served an important purpose for Carrie, whether she was conscious of it or not: they deepened the interdependence between them. She needed him for emotional and financial support, and he needed his mother's love for self-affirmation. Carrie undermined any hope for a healthy, reciprocal relationship by essentially eradicating their capability to adapt to the continued stressful events in their lives and by elevating their levels of anxiety.

Neither Carrie nor Langston was able to cope with their emotional highs and lows, and both often internalized the tension, stress, and anxiety to the point of becoming physically ill. In an undated letter circa 1936, Carrie finds herself in the throes of desperation as she writes: "I must have a little money by Monday for I don't know how I will be, will need some. I have been quite sick." After his break with Charlotte Osgood Mason, the patron who functions as an emotional surrogate for Carrie, Langston later recounted: "Violent anger makes me physically ill" (*Big Sea* 327). Rampersad is more pointed in connecting Langston's emotional state with physical repercussions: "Once again, as in the greatest moments of anxiety in his life, he felt his body poisoned, his limbs locking, the bones, especially in his left knee, hurting terribly" (ARI 393). These tendencies toward developing illnesses caused by stress are symptomatic of an inability to resolve issues by successfully forming cohesive relationships using what Bowen sets forth as problem-solving strategies.

All families have problems. The degree to which a family resolves the problems positively determines whether that family is functional. Effective problem solving requires family members to identify issues accurately, discuss those issues, and develop solutions or a coping mechanism. The family must be able to negotiate problems in a manner that allows every person to continue to function individually.

Another factor in determining the health of a family, according to Bowen, is the depth to which family members see themselves as emotionally close or distant—a measure based on the degree of bonding or cohesion among them. In such families, the *affect* can range from "smothering" each other to emotional absence. To be clear, bonding and cohesion certainly include such family support as involvement, shared interests, and mutual friends. But *over-involvement* is a pathway to problematic relations. Members of enmeshed families involve themselves in other family members' lives to the point that all lose their individuated personalities and the family unit develops diffused boundaries. As seen in the Hughes-Clark family, these members exhibit excessive emotional responses and have poorly differentiated family relationships. Disengaged families have more-rigid boundaries, walls separating them. Each member lacks emotional responsiveness and generally does not communicate well with the others. The results in both cases are serious problems with cohesion and bonding or, simply put, excessive conflict within the family.

In yet another way, such conflict or inappropriate emotional fusion causes diminished autonomous functioning in the family and increased emotional reactivity in interactions within the family. Members with this diminished capacity usually show a tendency to take undue responsibility for others to avoid assuming total responsibility for themselves. They help others to the neglect of themselves. Carrie's letters reveal that she, for example, makes herself totally responsible for her stepson—to the neglect of herself. Claiming total responsibility for the sustenance and well-being of Kit gives Carrie permission to complain about her poor living conditions. Indeed, she fuses her needs with his. One consequence of her actions is that she becomes almost totally self-focused, and the family, including Kit and Langston, exists only as a means to fulfill her various needs. Even as Kit ages and is able to work, for example, Carrie writes Langston aglow with the news that Kit loves her and generously shares his pay with her. The not-so-subtle intent is to induce guilt and coerce Langston into sending more money as further demonstrations of his love.

Carrie's letters show no indication of her having ever bonded appropriately with Langston, so apparently neither one of them ever became fully differentiated. Langston's extensive travels can be read as attempts to separate himself from Carrie and become more individuated, but he never reached full self-differentiation. He always needed his mother to love him. When she essentially abandoned him from the time he was a toddler, Carrie closed the door to any possibility of a strong family bond and cohesion. Still, his need to bond with her was always there. Sadly, even when they were together, in the midst of high tension, they were unable to talk meaningfully, let alone peacefully occupy the same space. Their *affect* illustrates a need to fuse and bond so that, paradoxically, they could stand alone and apart. That would never happen. When done *appropriately*, two people bond together to solve an impending problem, and both retain their individuation. When done *inappropriately*, they lose their individuation, as in the case of Carrie and Kit. Their inappropriate bonding led to inappropriate fusion, *triangulating* Langston into their relationship to help them cope.

Triangulation

Bowen tells us that *triangulation* is a common strategy in which two people include a third person to help them cope with their anxiety and emotional fusion. In citing one example of how the triangle works, Bowen discusses a husband whose relationship to his wife is "distant," thus predisposing her to a "relatively intense focus on the kids. Kept at arm's length by her husband, she devotes her emotional energy to the children, usually with the greatest intensity toward one particular child. This child may be the oldest son or daughter, or perhaps the one who looks like one of the parents" (qtd. in Gill 90). The role of this third person is to diffuse tension, usually by functioning as a diversion, collusive partner, or scapegoat for the other parties. It is possible that triangulation can have a positive effect by temporarily decreasing the anxiety and tension the couple often feels. It is just as likely that triangulation precipitates *more* conflict and stress, especially if the person triangulated into the relationship is one of the children.

Carrie often pulled Langston into her relationships with her husbands to help solve her problems. In this triangulation, the mother projects her unresolved feelings about an absent or ineffective husband onto her children, usually the oldest son. The son, in this case Langston, is expected to assume the role of parent-child. In projecting this role for Langston, Carrie demonstrates that she has little use for him until he becomes old enough to work and help her financially. She ignores his needs until Langston is able to serve as a source of support for her. As her needs increase, so do the demands she makes of him. Passive-aggressively, Carrie had long been triangulating Langston into her marriages as she received child support from James Hughes, which, for the most part, she used for her own benefit.[2] She became extremely angry with Langston for putting an end to this triangle and her financial windfall when he told his father to keep his money because he was no longer going to study at Columbia University. Ostensibly, Carrie is angry because Langston refuses a source of income *for her*. From a Bowen perspective, she is also angry because she loses control over that triangle. In using his personal power to end the triangulation with his father, Langston usurps Carrie's control over her relationship with him.

Carrie reestablishes her control when she triangulates Langston into her marriage with Homer. During Langston's teenage years, when Carrie and Homer are living together and seemingly getting along as they party, play cards, and socialize regularly, she triangulates Langston into this relationship because she still has unmet emotional needs. She essentially wants Langston to fulfill what Homer does not: her need to hear that she is loved. As an adult his role in the triangle shifts to a more mature one. For instance, she prepares for his visit by announcing to Homer that Langston will fix any problems they face, implying that Homer, her husband and theoretically the "head of the house," does not have the ability to do so. Upon Langston's arrival, Carrie gives Langston her marriage bed, forcing Homer to sleep with her in Gwyn's bed—the child's bed—or elsewhere. For Langston, this is undoubtedly a dubious "honor." For Homer, surely this is a form of emasculation. This gesture—by rendering one impotent and shaming the other—also becomes Carrie's way of punishing *both* of them for not providing adequately for her.

In Homer's absence and sometimes before he actually leaves, Carrie assures herself of someone to fulfill her financial and emotional needs by imploring Langston to come take care of her and Gwyn while Homer is away. Langston, in effect, is pulled into the triangle as the primary provider. In so doing Carrie elevates Langston from the role of child to a quasi husband. Once she positions Langston in that role, Carrie removes Homer from the triangle and essentially absolves him of his responsibility to provide for her and Gwyn, an absolution Homer gladly accepts.[3]

When the triangle is Carrie, Gwyn, and Langston, she becomes more demanding and insists that Langston provide not only subsistence needs, like food and shelter for herself and Gwyn, but also money to satisfy her desires to travel, make special donations to church fund-raising events, attend movies, and the like. In addition, she makes Langston primarily responsible for Gwyn's financial needs, including the frivolity of travel money for Gwyn to visit an out-of-town girlfriend.

The complex, troublesome emotions that Langston has for Carrie are real, deeply felt, and largely unrequited. Langston makes many failed attempts to create a solid connection with her, but never establishes an effective emotional link. By the same token, Carrie never realizes a healthy relationship with Langston, so she attempts to build a more emotionally rewarding one with Gwyn. She never achieves a balanced, reciprocal relationship with anyone, nor does she ever overcome the strong need to rely on others for her well-being and survival.

Bowen Family Systems Theory provides a cogent explanatory model for Carrie's many complications. The opportunities for Langston and Carrie to develop the needed familial interdependence were few. In the times they spent in each other's physical space, their interactions were usually caustic and turbulent. The heightened tension resulting from their physical distancing did not allow the healthy emotional bonding and cohesion that typically evolves to protect the family unit. Nevertheless, Langston held tightly to his need for his mother's love, if not the promise of love that she continually made and broke. Carrie, more matriarch than mother, tried, however perversely, to satisfy Langston's unfulfilled longings, but her version of the maternal fell short of the requisite remedy and thus she failed to rescue her "dear boy" from the loneliness and perhaps lovelessness that engulfed his life. As a woman with a poorly differentiated self, she is akin to the "doormat woman" that Guitar defines for Milkman Dead in Toni Morrison's *Song of Solomon*. Carrie was one of those

> women who had been spoiled children. Whose whims had been taken seriously by adults and who grew up to be the stingiest, greediest people on earth and out of their stinginess grew their stingy little love that ate everything in sight. They could not believe or accept the fact that they were unloved. They believed that the world itself was off balance when it appeared as though they were not loved. Why did they think they were so loveable? Why did they think their brand of love was better than, or even as good as, anybody else's? But they did. And they loved their love so much they would kill anybody who got in its way. (306)

Carrie, of course, kills no one. However, she certainly commits emotional "manslaughter" as she uses and manipulates her "dear boy" and others in the name of her love. It is a love that Morrison, again in *Song of Solomon*, describes as "anaconda love" (137), a predatory emotion that Storhoff uses to define *enmeshment*: "the suffocating bond parents occasionally create with their children" (291). It is this "love," for better or worse, that drives Carrie down the egocentric, domineering, but insecure pathway that defines her life.

NOTES

1. This discussion of "influence" is summarized more fully in John Edgar Tidwell, "Two Writers Sharing: Sterling A. Brown, Robert Frost, and 'In Dives' Dive,'" *African American Review* 31.3 (1997): 399–408.

2. In *The Big Sea*, Langston talks about his father raising his allowance while he was at Central High School. He then was able to help Carrie with household expenses (52). Having his allowance raised suggests that Langston was already getting one. Although this contradicts the notion of James being "a dead-beat dad," it still doesn't free him from the assertion that he was inappropriately fused with Langston.

3. After short moves away followed by reconciliations, Homer left Carrie for good. Clearly, he could not fuse effectively with Carrie and remain individuated. More probably, Homer reached a point where he just could no longer tolerate her self-centeredness, so he left Carrie with his son Gwyn permanently. Carrie writes Langston that she has to assume that Homer is dead as she hasn't heard from him for so long. With Homer's "death," Carrie's desire for greater familial interdependence with Langston collapses even further into an emotional relationship that, sadly, increases inappropriate enmeshment.

Langston Hughes as a baby, with mother, Carolyn Hughes. Printed by permission of Harold Ober Associates Incorporated. Copyright © 2013 by the Estate of Langston Hughes. Yale Collection of American Literature, Beinecke Rare Book and Manuscript Library.

Father, James Nathaniel Hughes. Printed by permission of Harold Ober Associates Incorporated. Copyright © 2013 by the Estate of Langston Hughes. Yale Collection of American Literature, Beinecke Rare Book and Manuscript Library.

Langston Hughes as young boy. Printed by permission of Harold Ober Associates Incorporated. Copyright © 2013 by the Estate of Langston Hughes. Yale Collection of American Literature, Beinecke Rare Book and Manuscript Library.

Langston Hughes's maternal grandmother, Mary Sampson Patterson Leary Langston.
Printed by permission of Harold Ober Associates Incorporated. Copyright © 2013
by the Estate of Langston Hughes. Yale Collection of American Literature, Beinecke
Rare Book and Manuscript Library.

Langston Hughes and family ca. 1916. *Left to right*: Langston, unidentified friend, stepfather Homer Clark, and Carrie. *Front right*: stepbrother Gwyn "Kit" Clark. Printed by permission of Harold Ober Associates Incorporated. Copyright © 2013 by the Estate of Langston Hughes. Yale Collection of American Literature, Beinecke Rare Book and Manuscript Library.

House in which Langston Hughes rented the attic bedroom ca. 1917. *Cleveland Plain Dealer*, August 23, 2010.

Mother and son at Langston Hughes's graduation from Lincoln University ca. 1929. Printed by permission of Harold Ober Associates Incorporated. Copyright © 2013 by the Estate of Langston Hughes. Yale Collection of American Literature, Beinecke Rare Book and Manuscript Library.

"Godmother," Charlotte Osgood Mason. Printed by permission of Harold Ober Associates Incorporated. Copyright © 2013 by the Estate of Langston Hughes. Yale Collection of American Literature, Beinecke Rare Book and Manuscript Library.

Mary McLeod Bethune ca. 1931. Printed by permission of Harold Ober Associates Incorporated. Copyright © 2013 by the Estate of Langston Hughes. Yale Collection of American Literature, Beinecke Rare Book and Manuscript Library.

Gwyn Clark, "To Lang Sincerely Kit," ca. 1937. Printed by permission of Harold
Ober Associates Incorporated. Copyright © 2013 by the Estate of Langston Hughes.
Yale Collection of American Literature, Beinecke Rare Book and Manuscript Library.

Langston Hughes, with family friend Toy Harper at piano. Printed by permission of Harold Ober Associates Incorporated. Copyright © 2013 by the Estate of Langston Hughes. Yale Collection of American Literature, Beinecke Rare Book and Manuscript Library.

Langston Hughes. Printed by permission of Harold Ober Associates Incorporated. Copyright © 2013 by the Estate of Langston Hughes. Yale Collection of American Literature, Beinecke Rare Book and Manuscript Library.

The Letters

Dreams Deferred
1926–1929

The letters in this period effectively comprise an introduction, framing a number of themes, issues, and problems that Carrie develops in subsequent correspondence. Implicitly, they record a subtle erosion of her optimism about life and the many dreams she held out for success on her own terms. What unfolds is her deepening realization of how she must depend on others for simple subsistence and her reckoning with a loss of personal freedom. Instead of the self-sufficiency that comes with being fully individuated, Carrie must turn to various forms of fusion to ensure her survival. She has a growing sense that others are responsible, even obligated, to take care of her. The letters in this section lay a foundation for understanding the strategies she employs to encourage the kind of emotional relationships that will enable her to feel good about herself. She does not write deliberately or self-consciously, as if she is trying to work out her feelings, achieve self-knowledge, or create a document for posterity. Nevertheless, she paints a remarkable self-portrait that defines her persona, especially insofar as it relates to the family. In turn, we are able to intuit the family's response to her.

Many of the letters vacillate between two modes of expression. Either they read like lists detailing information about family and friends or they convey business matters. The tone is generally aloof, if not unemotional, revealing few of Carrie's deepest feelings. She tells us, for instance, that friends take her to shows and dinner or even send for her to come to a funeral. Carrie appears to be gracious and grateful for the well-meant generosity of her friends, but there is little to indicate humility or her heartfelt appreciation for their kindness. This is one of her methods of manipulation. She exchanges her gratitude for the services that people provide her. She feels a sense of entitlement and privilege and creates a very deliberate strategy of exchanging her gratitude and love for providing for her needs and for fulfilling her wishes. Of course, her donors' largesse affects her self-esteem. Instead of feeling fulfilled and good about who she is, she rationalizes the proud person she was meant to be and therefore makes herself feel she deserves the good offices of her friends and family. Carrie never talks about having earned their support. Her discussions, instead, are about her entitlement through the good works of her father and other family members.

In other moments, she resorts to importuning to solicit and express love. For instance, when she writes to Langston about her need for money for a trip and a coat, she abruptly shifts to an emotional appeal and puts their relationship on the line. For him not to accede to her demands translates to his being at fault for the lacunae in their relationship: "I want you to help me this time and I won't bother you ever again. Dear, why don't you love me. Why aren't we more loving and chummy." The spontaneity of the query about their relationship does not indicate a planned or orchestrated motive. It does suggest a willfulness, as if an emotional need, emanating from somewhere in the wellspring of her heart, suddenly required unbidden expression. Her question, in effect, becomes a form of manipulation since it further entraps Langston, demanding that he show his affection for her in the way she recognizes best—materially.

She also tends to hold him hostage emotionally by placing their relationship next to others, particularly with her stepson Gwyn "Kit" Clark, as a way to demonstrate to Langston that he has not earned the favored position. She forces him to confront the great estimate she has of others, especially her image of Gwyn as a "good hearted kid." The obvious implication—that Langston is not as good as Gwyn—is calculated to prick Langston's conscience. On one occasion, when Gwyn works at a golf course, he brings his earnings, eighty cents, home to Carrie. That she lavishes so much praise on him for such a modest gift is intended to make Langston jealous. It sets up a competition between the two sons that obligates Langston to match Gwyn's magnanimity. No doubt it was as transparent to Langston as it is to today's reader when Carrie follows that by stating she has to buy Gwyn shoes that day. Carrie's inappropriate emotional fusion with Gwyn is surprising but obviously important. As she would later write: "Gwyn is all I have that holds me together." Carrie further exemplifies her needs after Charlotte Osgood Mason, through Alain Locke, sets up Gwyn in a boarding house so that he can attend school in the Northeast. The arrangement was designed to alleviate some of the financial and emotional strain on Langston. Carrie sabotages the whole arrangement simply because she is lonely and needs to be close to Gwyn. She is also jealous that Gwyn has become attached to Eva Stokien, the owner of the boarding house. Rather than have Gwyn too emotionally near another woman, she removes him from school and a setting in which he has seemingly thrived.

This section, then, introduces the multifaceted character that defines Carrie.

Washington D.C.

Feby 24th [1926]

My Dear Boy:

Your dearest letter came. I had waited so long for it.

Gwyn and I are well, except Gwyn says his tonsils feel just like they have just been took out.

I put my glasses in my pocket on Washington's birthday and Mrs. Colin & I were going out & I swung my pocket against the fence and broke the glasses. Poor me always doing bad luck to my self. Ha! Ha! I am sending you a review by Mrs. Johnson[1] which came in an open letter that had been all over every where. So I am sending the contents in mine.

What do you think. We have two cats up here tonight. Our old one then a new stray kitten. You should see them. They get on famously.

Thanks for the $. I never needed it worse I missed two days this week.

Buster still takes his usual lung exercise. Wah-wah all day. We have a bride & groom with us in your room *green* I am afraid the cows will bite there heads off if they go by a pasture. Poor things think they are happy. Don't know of the last war at all. It is case "where ignorance is bliss &ct."

Your box is there I know by now dear heart.

I could not get it off until Tues—as it was to late Sat, when Gwyn came home.

Write when you can.

Mrs. Hilyer was over Mon.

Yours Mother

1. Georgia Douglas Johnson (1886–1966) moved to Washington, D.C., in 1910, where she earned the reputation of being the foremost poet among the women of the Harlem Renaissance. She and her husband, Henry Lincoln Johnson, opened their home, called "Halfway House," as a gathering place for Black intellectuals and artists. Her Saturday night literary salon was a welcome retreat for Hughes and other artists.

Washington, D.C.
March 27, 1926

Dearest boy,

I am writing up to the House and Mary Alice[1] is holding to my knee, saying, "googan—googan," I don't know what she says at all. Her language is past me most of the time. I am also trying to make a lemon pie on the side. I had a bad sick spell today and don't feel just right yet.

I wanted to ask your opinion about going to Cleveland. I can go when you do or on the 17th, that is I guess I will have car fare and little over. What do you expect to make up there? I'd love to come there to see you, but of course, unless you had a little money I might not have enough to last until I get a job. I am anxious to go over to Cleveland as all of the crowd wants me to come back. If you think I had better go then let me know, if not I will wait later. Will you spend your vacation there or N.Y. or here? The work is getting so hard up to Kennedy's. I must try a change. Write what you think. I am hungry to see you. Love. Love. Kisses. Mother.

Gwyn went out to Golf links today. Only made 80¢. But he gave it to me. He is one good hearted kid. I had to get him some shoes tonight though.

1. Daughter of the White people, the Kennedy family for whom Carrie did babysitting and domestic work.

---

36 N. Ind.
Atlantic City, New Jersey
Nov 3rd [1926]

My Dear Boy:—

I am just mailing you a box with a cake. I hope you will enjoy it. I made your favorite cake I hope.

Will you come down this week end? I have a nice room and I think you would enjoy the stay. Let [me] know. I am crazy to see you, you know. Gwyn had quick [*sic*] a sick spell on Monday. But he is better now. I enjoyed "Nigger Heaven"[1] very much and it is our people to a "T." Your blurb in the Opportunity[2] was quite catchy. I will be glad when I get them on the phonograph. I want a machine but can't get $25.00 together to get one seems like.

Write when you can to me. I am always glad to [have] heard [from you]. Pearl was so sad because I moved but I had no advantage at all there. No light, nor heat, back room.

Love to you from Gwyn and I

Yours lovingly
Ma

1. A novel loosely based on the socioeconomic classes of Black Harlem written by Carl Van Vechten, a White music critic, photographer, and close friend of Langston Hughes. The novel was criticized more for its unfortunate title than for the mediocre writing. Van Vechten paid Hughes one hundred dollars to write blues lyrics for *Nigger Heaven*'s second edition to replace the ones he had published without permission.

2. Subtitled *A Journal of Negro Life, Opportunity* was the monthly magazine of the National Urban League. It was published 1923–49.

———————

Atlantic City, N. J.
Tuesday

Dearest Boy:

Mother's Darling Boy:—Oh! I wish I could see you tonight. I am lonely. Oh! So lonesome to see you. It seems that I am getting old and I have never seen you very much. You & I are most always apart. May be that is the way of the world. It is best to only see a little of those we love best! But everyone sees you more than I do. Being close to you don't do much good. I'd see you about as often (once a year) if I was out west or any where.

Was it not sad about Clarissa Scott's death?[1] Mrs. Scott is here on a visit to her daughter. I thought I would possibly drop by to see her.

Gwyn is yet doing nothing in school. He don't seem to have any ambition to learn any thing but read all the time. Prof. Smith just told me Gwyn could learn & keep up with his class if he would. I wish you'd write him a letter and urge him to try won't you? He is affected by what you say and seems to want to please you. He and I have arguments now & can wish you were here. We are playing the Vick [Victrola gramophone]. We have a very pretty Pipe organ recital "Honorable Moon" & "Just a Song at Twilight." They are very pretty. We have Clara Smith[2] singing "Dogone lazy Man" and "I Don't love Nobody," it's very sad and dreary. I know you'd like it.

Say you couldn't come down next week end could you. There is some one lives here, who comes down nearly every week I see by the paper. Do they drive? If so couldn't you sneak down with them once in a while.

I got a lovely letter from Zora[3] asking me to live with her in N.Y. Such a lovely letter. I loved her so full hearted, not a stinted word. I may go over there on my vacation. Miss Laura will be back Nov. 1st and I don't think I will stay as it will not be pleasant I am sure. Mrs. Hay has asked me to stay she says she can't bear me to quit, but she don't have to work with Laura and I do. I know what it means.

Well I know you are tired of reading now and I will just stop. Come down soon as you can. I will always hold your fare back home. Mrs. Rhone asked kindly for you. Pearl is looking for you down Gwyn going to several parties.

Write me I am so loncsome

Your Mother

Did you ever hear from James Hughes.

> *Dying Child's Dream*
> I see a man in a brilliant blaze of light
> He wears a robe of white,
> And his hair is long and yellow.
> I wonder who can be this fellow!

With open arms he looks straight at me,
At last I have it. It is the Lord Jesus
Coming after me.
Am I ready Ah! Yes
And I will go willingly.
  (For Langston)

1. Clarissa Scott Delaney was a young poet Langston had met in New York. She was married to attorney Hubert Delaney for just a year, when kidney disease took her life on October 11, 1927.

2. Smith (1894–1935) was considered by many as second only to famed blues singer Bessie Smith, with whom she worked. The two were not related. Clara was often billed as "the Queen of the Moaners."

3. Zora Neale Hurston (1891–1960), born in Notasulga, Alabama, claimed Eatonville, Florida, as her home. This all-Black town served as the setting for most of her folklore, plays, essays, and fiction. Initially Carrie liked Zora and felt that Zora respected her and her home until Zora came to visit an ailing Langston and confronted him about the ownership rights to the play *Mule Bone*. As a very rude Zora was leaving without saying good-bye, an angry Carrie "pursued Miss Hurston into the hall to give her a piece of her mind" (*Big Sea* 333). Langston had to get out of his sickbed to restrain his mother.

———————

New York

Dearest Boy,

Your letter came and found me well but very very busy as I was just quitting my job and had lots to do. But I did not quit my job, I only came to take a vacation and come back to work about Sept 7th. But when I come back I will not sleep in, but just work there just the same. It's good to have a job to come back to eh? I am leaving by bus Sat and hope to stay over in Cleveland at least a day or two.

The bus makes the same time the train does and I can't believe it myself but I went on and sat down and the comfort is marvelous—more than a police car seat. Now darling be good. I will write you at my first stop and let you know how I get along. Love by the bushel to you. Kisses galore. There is a party for me tomorrow night. I am so tired. I love you and love you. Yours Ma.

———————————

[1928]

Dear Langston

Enclosed please find letter from Mrs. Stokens.[1] This is the 3rd one she sent me, all imply that she does not particular want Gwyn. Gwyn says she nags him so that he can't stay with her. Now I am leaving it all to you. Could Gwyn go to border? Aberdeen town is cheaper also. And nice climb or Downing town its $2.00 per month. Let me know at once so I can get him off some where. I do not believe he will do any good now as he seems disgusted with Mrs. Stokens.

Ans at once.

Can't you come down this weekend.

1. Eva Stokien was the woman in Springfield, Massachusetts, who provided room and board to Gwyn Clark and sent him to school. This arrangement was made by Alain Locke, at the behest and largesse of Charlotte Osgood Mason. Carrie very much resented this arrangement and complained that she never heard from Gwyn. Mrs. Stokien wrote her that he was fine and had friends and that the boys were more interested in their marbles than in writing letters. Carrie sabotaged the arrangement and refused to let him go back for the fall semester.

———————————

Sunday [1928]

Dear Mrs. Clark

I received a letter from Mr. Clarke saying that you could send Gwyn by the first of Sept. School will open on Thursday the forth. You had better send him on Saturday or Sunday as Monday will be so crowded. I am so very lame can hardly stand on my feet. Hope that you will soon be settled in a nice place. Glad that you write Dr. DeBerry. He may can find a place in the activities of the church. I do hope so. That you may be near your boy. I feel very much for you as both of your loved ones are away from you. Glad that Gwyn is enjoying himself. It will not spoil him. I know he is having his own way from you. I have not given up my trip to Brooklyn. I may come at any time. My sister in law wants me to come before the children go back to school. I am not able to use my legs. I don't like N.Y. City and don't want to stay for one month. I have a brother in the city. I only go and call on him as I hate the city. I am a small town guy. Well, I hope your boy will come back looking fine.

Le me know when he is coming. Tell him all the boys wants him home. I don't see any of the girls as I cannot get out.

Hoping you can read this as my hands are so lame.

I am yours
Eva Stokien.

P.S. Let me know if Gwyn wants to come back. It would be very hard to have him come and he don't want to.

———————

New York, N.Y.
[Oct. 29, 1928]
Monday

Dear Langston,

When you read the contents of this letter you will smile. I can see you— It's been years since I've felt so interested, and I am almost happy. I got a letter from Sherman Harvey[1] last night and he tells me the 39th meeting of the Inter State literary of Kansas and the West,[2] which my father organized and only a few of the ones then present are there now. I want to go as it meets in Lawrence Kansas, my home, December 28–30th—and *can* go if you could only help me buy a coat. Can you? Or rather will you? Instead of giving me a Xmas present could you give me $15.00 between now and then on a coat? Oh! Langston you don't know how bad I want to go to the meeting. I'd love to take you. But I can take your books and sell them there and I know I'd do well with them.

Dear Heart, we never agree on anything but please be interested in this, for I am so interested in it and I don't want you to discourage the idea, please don't. Will you? At Xmas time I think there will be rates, if so I'll go on train if not by Bus one way, and one on train. I have plenty of clothes save coat. I want you to help me this time and I won't bother you ever again. Dear, why don't you love me. Why aren't we more loving and chummy. Why don't you ever confide in me. I know I have no sense to help you in your work but I'd enjoy your confidence. Now Langston, I have no one else to talk to, you will agree with me and help me won't you if you can? Please don't be angry because I want to go, for I'd see everyone I ever knew so I am wild to go, and I will have the money. The Bus leaves here makes Pittsburg in one day, the next makes Indianapolis and then on to K.C. 2 days and 1 night that's not much worse than train. Please don't dampen my ardor write an encouraging letter won't you?

I am sending Gwyn's overcoat this week. I am afraid its cold up there. Please write at once. I am over excited about the prospect of going but can't go without a coat. I have three nice dresses. But *must* [double-underlined] have a coat. I can get someone in my place for one or two weeks very well. Come back to the Johnsons.[3] Please write me won't you. Oh! If you could meet this meeting of learned men of the U.S. that your grandfather organized. I'd be so proud for you.

Could I sell copies of your songs out there too.

Write. Yours,
Mother

1. A man that Carrie had grown up with in Lawrence. The *Historic Times* (September 26, 1891), a local Black newspaper, touted Harvey as "a credit to any community and certainly the pride of Lawrence." He was also known as "the silver-tongued orator."

2. Literary society founded by Carrie's father, Charles Howard Langston, in Lawrence, Kansas, in 1891.

3. Carrie's employers, for whom she was a live-in maid and housekeeper.

———————

New York, N Y
November 19th [1928]

Dear Boy, I am just very sad, I went to Atlantic City yesterday as my friend Nettie died, and the family sent for me to come. Poor girl. I just heard from her Monday and Tuesday I got the message she was dead. I felt terrible over it for I did like her so much. Poor Mrs. Strong is all broken up over it and she hugged me and told me she would miss me more than ever now. How are you? I went down and picked out a $40 coat and paid $5 down on it. So when you are ready, I will pay on it then get it out. Do you think that is too much? I told you Irma was here did I not? I love her here. It's lots of company. Let me hear from you soon, won't you? Sorry you are not coming down Thanksgiving but you will be down soon after won't you?

Much love,
Mother.

———————

[Jan 7, 1929]
N Y, NY
Sunday Eve

My Dearest Baby,

You will be surprised, when I tell you, that I went to hear Roland Hayes[1] today and it was just wonderful. Oh! he is marvelous. Miss Brown Delau took me then I went to dinner with her and Anna Mae and we had a very nice time. I shook hands with Mr. Hayes and he sent his kindest love to you and says he hopes you will be successful in school. He was so very nice. I am out of a job. I knew I was going to lose that job and I did. But I am trying for another now. Be darling & sweet. Hope to see you some day soon.

Dearest good night.
Your mother.

1. Roland Hayes (1887–1976) was an accomplished tenor, whose phenomenal success in Europe and at home symbolized the potential of the New Negro artists of the Harlem Renaissance. Hayes began his musical career with the Fisk Jubilee Singers in 1911.

———————————

New York
Feb 1st [1929]

Dearest Son—

One more milestone, one more year to your record. Dear One may you always know naught but joy and your path strewn with blessings, good wishes, love and peace. May you never know real sorrow, but instead so live that contentment will crown your whole life.

Fame and fortune must be yours, to be approved and admired has also been your portion, your wonderful personality has made you many friends and benefactors. You have lived above slander, and life for you is a clean page, to make or mar it as you will. In your grasp is wealth, influence, position, fame, love and friendships and I hope they become yours for aye.

Mother's love and prayers are for many happy returns of this day, for her only darling son. For in spite of all, you are *mine* and I do faithfully love you and dearly, passionately love you even if I can't show it to you. Oh, I wish I was able to do wonders for you, but being poor is absolutely an irrevocable fact so can't help you any at all, but I'd love to do so. Now come down when you can. Helen sent you a wine. I sent you the cake. Helen's birthday is Monday.

Write me soon darling,

Your Mother—
C——

———————————

[1929]
New York
3054 Godwin Terrace

My Dearest Boy: Just got your letter and I was going to write and tell you what a nice affair it was Monday night and everyone I met regretted so much you was not there and Hall[1] said he was sorry you could not have heard your songs—for they sure went over "big." Both of them getting encores and "Fire" by the little Warner fellow was great. They applauded & shouted. Wish you'd been there. The house was crowded.[2] Boxes. Loges & floor. They danced, of course. Hall's singers did beside the regular spirituals "St. Louis Blues,"[3] it was wonderful. "Hush A Bye," "Casey Jones," sorry I did not have a program. They sold for 10¢ and I happened to be very, very short of money Monday so did not buy one—but may be able to get one for you. Am going to Mrs. Berry's for dinner the 4th. She said she wish you were here. And I am so sorry you are way up there alone. Are you very lonely? Jackie said tell you he thought he would be up to Lincoln [University] to spend the day with you one day next week as he was going to Philly on business. I saw Jimmie Allen and he said he had your desk photo finished and would send it to you. *You know when?* Dr. Locke[4] was there and told me he had trouble with his heart. He does not look or feel well. He could not dance. I saw Bruce[5] also. Very English you know with several changes—shirt and tie. He was not there long enough to turn around good but he's very English Ha! Ha! He said English people had no conception at all of "Porgie."[6] I told him so what in the world did English know of "Harlem and its Negroes." He laughed and laughed over it.

Langston, I wish you'd seen this kid I nurse. She is the cutest kid you ever saw. She is already been asked for [by] the movies. The people want to take her now to Hollywood. Her grandmother is there with some movie people & a man Sunday just begged Mrs. Jaffe to allow him to enter Phyllis—her eyes, her facial expressions, her intelligence is wonderful. Wish you could have seen her.

Well, so you again heard from Mexico. Of course your father has also seen of your success. I am so glad. You will answer those old souls of course. I am of the opinion that God has been very, *very* good to you & I even though we have been wicked, he has blessed us wonderfully. Just to think, although I have had to work hard, glad I could. I lived to be made very, very exceedingly happy to see you graduate from college. Oh! Langston I was so proud, so happy over you and for you.

Thanks for the offer to help me go to Kansas. The fare by train is $48.50, by Bus $28.50. I want to leave here about Aug 7th. I had planned to try the bus, and if I don't care for the trip I can take the train at Cleveland or Indianapolis, which ever way I go.

This woman here wants me to take one months vacation then come back to her. I may but I am so tired of the child. I am nearly crazy some times. Yes Gwyn says Tante says that's his home always and that he must always come there yet.

Well, I guess I've said everything. Hope you much success in your work.

Yours truly, Mamma.

1. Hall Johnson (1888–1970) was a skilled musician who studied at the New York Institute of Music, the Juilliard School, and the Philadelphia Music Academy and who received acclaim in the 1920s for his musical compositions and for the Hall Johnson Choir. Johnson produced *Run, Little Chillun* (1933), a folk drama indebted to the works of Zora Neale Hurston. The show had a profitable 126-performance run during the Great Depression.

2. Edith J. R. Isaacs wrote that "a Negro Theater is not alone a theater in which the players are all Negroes—singers, dancers, composers, comedians like the Williams and Walker companies—or one playing to a Negro audience, like the Lafayette Theater in Harlem. It is not a theater dedicated to plays of Negro life, like Paul Green's *In Abraham's Bosom*, or Marc Connelly's *The Green Pastures*, or to plays by Negro authors, like Langston Hughes's *Mulatto* or Richard Wright's *Native Son*. Rather it is a theater in which the best elements of all of these combine to interpret the Negro, every kind of Negro—his life and his talents, his gifts and his burdens, his racial heritage and his personal achievements, to interpret all of this to the Negro himself and to his fellow Americans" (495).

3. Written by W. C. Handy (1873–1958), who was arguably the most famous composer associated with the blues form.

4. Alain Locke (1885–1954), in a 1935 psychograph, proclaimed himself to be the "philosophical midwife" to the Harlem generation of younger writers. Critic, educator, philosopher, and mentor to Langston Hughes and other artists of the era, he taught at Howard University.

5. Richard Bruce Nugent (1906–87) was a writer and artist of the Harlem Renaissance. In 1926 with Wallace Thurman, Langston Hughes, Zora Neale Hurston, Aaron Douglas, and

others, he founded the one-issue literary magazine *Fire!!* His novel excerpt, "Smoke, Lilies, and Jade," was the first openly homosexual writing published by an African American.

6. Carrie probably meant *Porgy* (1927), the play written by White authors DuBose and Dorothy Heyward. *Porgy & Bess*, a folk opera written by DuBose Heyward, George Gershwin, and Ira Gershwin, did not open until October 10, 1935.

Zenith and Descent
1930–1934

The correspondence in these five years records the long, arduous journey culminating in Carrie achieving the one shining moment in her adult life: her successful appearance on stage as an actress. Inasmuch as the letters document the pinnacle of her happiness, they also reveal empathy-inducing narratives of her descent into a valley of desperation, poverty, loneliness, and despair. Her determined rise and precipitous fall are more than a personal odyssey: they are emotional experiences undertaken by her entire family, both immediate and extended.

Before and following her stage appearance, Carrie impresses upon Langston that loneliness is her constant companion. At times, she states it simply: "I am lonely." The sheer simplicity of the statement powerfully evokes pathos and portrays a heartfelt, tender moment. More protracted, dramatic expressions effectively heighten her emotional emphasis: "All of Life is such a muddle. I don't know what to do or say, and I am old and a pauper, and no use to anyone. I am just about given up the struggle." This fatalistic excerpt represents one of the times Carrie effectively meditates on the meaning of her life. On Mother's Day 1933, she essentially denies the reality of their relationship as she ruminates in a letter to Langston about the quality of her own performance as mother: "Langston, today made me wonder have I been all a Mother could be to you & Gwyn. I mean a poor Mother? Does it seem to you that I have been all the name implies, some time I feel you & I were never as close. Heart & heart as we should be, but I have loved you very dearly and if I failed in some things it was lack of knowledge." The introspection cuts both ways. This moment of self-reflection becomes an instance of stock taking, in which she assesses her life and how well she has acquitted herself as a mother. The passage is also a plea for a sign of affirmation. Carrie, like most poorly differentiated people, desperately needs the approval of others. Here she seeks Langston's approbation.

In quite another way, Carrie summons up a burst of emotion that demonstrates the possibility that she had at least *intended* to be a good mother. When the relationship between Langston and "Godmother" (as he called Charlotte Osgood Mason) collapses into disrepair, he identifies his resulting psychosomatic illness as a case of tapeworms. Carrie writes with all the fervor of a frantic mother on the verge of losing her child to death: "No matter what kind of engagements you have the best thing for you to do is come here to Mothers house and heal and be where I can wait on you, and take care of you fix you the right kind of food and save you your rent and expense until you are well. I can get you a good doctor here. . . . Come and get well. Now darling, mother wants you to do this for I know it is for the best. You would get well quicker. I can make you very comfortable." Eventually he relents and returns to Cleveland where Carrie "mothers" him and provides for his well-being. From a Bowen perspective, her introspection effectively creates enmeshment in their relationship. True to her nature, she mentions the financial aspects of his coming to her to heal. She offers to save him his rent and expense until he gets well.

No doubt Langston himself is desperate for the nursing care that Carrie can provide and, more importantly, for some attention from his mother. But if he ultimately seems unappreciative, the reason probably derives from her persistent efforts to bring him into the fold as a household provider. In getting him home, she manages to triangulate him into her relationships with Homer and Gwyn. The peripatetic Homer is in and out of Carrie's home and life so much that she appeals to Langston for the financial and emotional support a husband and father should provide. In Homer's absence, Carrie repeats a tiresome plea for Langston to return home and care for her and Gwyn. When Gwyn grows into adulthood, Carrie consistently babies him and appeals to Langston to help provide for Gwyn's welfare.

Langston's role in the family thus transforms from being the son to that of surrogate provider. In this position, he is fused into the family to ease the tensions brought about by a horrendous economic climate. Even though he did his best to meet Carrie's definition of his place in the family, the role she creates for him is inappropriate. It is small wonder that, in order to preserve himself, Langston generally deals with these entreaties by distancing himself physically and emotionally as far from Carrie as possible. She does her best, however, to make it difficult for him to maintain that distance and to say no. Lines such as "Langston, it is so lovely to be known as your mother" are flattering and perhaps tempting. In the long run, they are not persuasive enough to make him do more than he feels duty-bound to do. In any case, whether he does something for her or not, she demands more, even though it exceeds what he is capable of doing.

Sandwiched between inappropriate fusion and triangulation is Carrie's moment of greatest self-fulfillment: her starring role in Hall Johnson's successful musical *Run, Little Chillun*. She exclaims: "Yes, your mother is an actress at last, the dream I dreamed as a little child is very near realized. I *am* one of the principals in Hall Johnson's show 'Run Little Chillun Run.'" She shares the stage with Freddie Washington, Austin Burleigh, Edna Thomas, Lillie King, and DeWitt Spencer—all renowned Black performers of that day. The ultimate confirmation of the show's success occurs when, as Carrie writes, Gloria Swanson, Carl Van Vechten, Charlie Chaplin, and other White luminaries "pronounced it marvelous." In the several months from late 1932 to early 1933, she relives the feeling she once enjoyed as a Belle of Black Lawrence. It is a heady time for Carrie and she feels on top of the world. The Depression, spreading economic desperation like wildfire, eventually claims the show too, and Carrie finds herself rudely thrust back into the malaise that had come to define her adult life.

Throughout the bad and good times, she never strays too far from dysfunctional strategies she uses in attempts to make her family functional. As the letters here reveal, poor self-individuation, inappropriate enmeshment, and triangulation are means by which she seeks to give her life meaning. As discussed in the epilogue, Langston's response to Carrie in such works as *Soul Gone Home* did not reward her attempts at motherhood with the applause and appreciation she desperately needs.

36 N. Ind.

Atlantic City, New Jersey

Feby 1st

Dearest Boy: Can it be your birthday and I am without any funds to give you even a card. But Darling son, I will certainly send you this line to tell you that Mother remembers it, and hopes you may have many more.

All the joy, the Fame, the honor, the happiness, the sunshine, without the shadows, every conceivable pleasure, goodness and greatness, may they be for you in abundance.

Frank[1] left again today for Tenn. His mother is very ill again.

Gwyn is anxious to come see you.

Regards to Mr. Roy, Tate, Brown, Day & all.

Your Mother

1. Frank Madison was one of Carrie's many cousins.

Will send your things now

Atlantic City, N.J.

Dear Langston: You are getting the first paper out of the box. I can't tell you exactly how I feel over your letter, but I don't want Gwyn way off some where and with people I do not know[1] and he is not well and Gwyn is all I have that holds me together. I am so lonely, so discouraged, so tired, so disgusted generally I don't believe I want Gwyn to go away from me.

As I tried to tell you the job is unbearable. I am just sticking by a thread. Constant bickering. Every one on edge and I am sick of it all. (Enclosed find Uncle Dess's[2] letter.) I belief I would like the change if I could get out there.

Now if I had about thirty dollars after I got there I could live a month or so without worry. Stay out there a year or so and I guess by that time I could get back and leave Gwyn with his people if he cared to stay. What do you think? If not I will stop the job that pays $50.00 and go somewhere nearer and work out my [own] salvation.

Langston it was so kind of you to interest your self and I do thank you but I don't see how I could stand to have Gwyn away. You can't realize, being young and out with people and happy, how lonely a person like me is and come home to no one. I tell you, I guess. I'm getting old but I could not stand to be any lonlier than I am. So please don't think I am ungrateful for I am. But I can't see that separation just now if I can do better. I must work so I must go somewhere where it can be obtained. Do you know anything about Lakewood? They say there's lots of work there? I hate to go so far from you, but what can I do. I can't stay on this job so why fail to get the $50.00.

Write me at once, by Tuesday and let me know what you think.

Gwyn don't pass until June.

Yours,
Mother

1. He was with Eva Stokien in Springfield, Massachusetts, in 1928.
2. Desalines Langston, Carrie's stepbrother, was a barber in Kansas City, Missouri.

Atlantic City
Monday Eve

Dear Langston:

I just got your letter. Glad you enjoyed the box. Now I will send Gwyn some little Easter token if I am better. One week ago I burned my knee. I means a nasty bad burn, so I have been so I could scarcely get around, then Saturday I took a terrible cold, so I am all in. I am sick today and am lonely and tired, no one to do one thing for me. I'd go to N.Y. tomorrow if I was able but I fear that terrible loneliness there, no one. I am ashamed to feel so but—I can't help it any more.

Enclosed find three dollars. Mrs. Hill bought each of your books again. Send with verse from your poems with your autograph, put for

Mrs. Helen Wright,

Autograph both books. Send to

> Mrs. Wm. Sturd Hill
> 2400—16th St. N.W.
> Washington, D.C.

Send soon as you can. I am keeping $1.00 as I was sick and may need it. Will send it later when you are really broke. I do wish I could go to Gen Conference[1] at Kansas City, May 20th. There will be rates but I am so poor.

No, I have no shoes yet.

Miss Laura appreciated your letter very much. She is the same cat one day good and the next——.

I'm sorry I wrote this letter, would tear it up if I did not have about the books in it.

I am leaving Atlantic City very soon, contention at work all the time, this blame dull room every night every one in bed at 8.30. It is giving me the creeps.

Don't answer this letter at all.

Your mother is full of self pity tonight.

---

1. At this yearly conference of the African Methodist Episcopal Church, bishops appoint ministers to their churches.

———————

> Atlantic City, N.J.
> Sat
> [June 1930]

Well, Son. Monday 16th I will be through out to Madame Hays and I do not care. I am sick of it all. Hard tiresome work, constant, under the hardest task master—and constant wranglings and words. Oh! I'm sick of it.

Never knowing where you stand. So Mrs. Hay told me I'd better go away, next Monday. In a way it's a dismissal. But she has made her deposit smaller. Says she fears she can only give me $25.00. Now what shall I do?

I will see you in Philly any how no matter where I go.

Gwyn is not well and must get away from here soon. I do wish I was rich for 1 day. Don't you? What would it cost to send him to Mass? How far & all.

Yours Mother

So sorry you could not come.

Atlantic City

My Dear Boy

Did you get the cake and cigarettes? I hope all o.k. I am just dead tired. I can hardly go any longer say Langston, I hate to ask you a favor, after all you have done, but I am right up to the place I can't go no further.

I got Gwyn a suite. He had to have one, I owe $6.00 on it, I owe $4.00 on my dress. I pledged $2.00 on this St. Augustine Church. My Insurance[1] was over due and I can't pay it this week, so I have to appeal to you. Can you lend me a few dollars and I can pay you back almost any time you need it.

Will you do this for me right away and I will pay you back. When ever you need it. I have got to leave Atlantic City. Gwyn has begun with a cold, and Langston he is so thin. I am sick of this job the Negroes here have got sickening. It's a fuss and a wrangle every day.

You can get the shawl[2] whenever you send for it. Hope you enjoyed the cake, these darkies here are tell Mrs. Hay everything doing all they can to put her against me. Of course I don't care for I am just dead tired. Please help me out now and I won't forget it.

Your loving Mother

1. Carrie let her life insurance lapse. At her death Langston borrowed money from Carl Van Vechten to bury her and went into debt to the mortuary. Later, Mamie L. Anderson Pratt, the funeral director, wrote several letters and visited his home to collect the $107.76 balance of the $257.34 cost of the funeral services, which included casket, embalming, grave, hearse, and limousine. She appealed to the traditional mother-child relationship, which Carrie and Langston's was not: "Now, please let me have my money. I am so surprised from one Whom lost the dearest friend on earth (Mother) and will not pay her

funeral bill." Langston returned to her good graces when he explained to her that his agents were supposed to have sent royalties from his play *Mulatto* to cover the balance.

2. From a friend, Mary Leary Langston received the bullet-riddled, bloodstained shawl worn by her first husband, Lewis Sheridan Leary, when he was critically wounded at the raid on Harper's Ferry Federal Arsenal with abolitionist John Brown. He later died at a farmhouse where he was taken in and treated. Former president Teddy Roosevelt honored her at a commemorative ceremony in Osawatomie, Kansas, where he delivered his re-nowned "New Nationalism" speech, on August 31, 1910. Langston donated the shawl to the Ohio State Archaeological and Historical Society in Columbus, Ohio, on May 10, 1943.

[Sept 8, 1930]
Cleveland, Ohio
Monday

My Dear Langston,

Just the dullest Sunday I ever spent here. This place is a regular bore. Dull—gloomy, lonesome. A perfect pain is this dump.

Gwyn is supposed to start to school tomorrow. I am sure Gwyn did not pass as his transfer says fail.[1] So I am thoroughly discouraged over his school. He is not the least interested, just plays all the time.

As yet Homer has not been able to make a fire,[2] so is only getting the little $10 per and we are very short yet, but maybe it will get cold after while.

I have sold three books and have some promised. I will let you know when I need more. The library here wants you to send the library an auto-graphed copy of your book. She said that Dubois,[3] Johnson[4] &tc sent an autographed copy to the library. So do as you like about it and the stores here sold out your books and were waiting for more this week.

The library has three copies just shelved yesterday. Homer and Gwyn is working on the football. Dear, I wish you were down here for a while for Gwyn would love the guest I guess. We had lemon pie the other day. Gwyn got his shoes with the money he had. He has not the wheels yet. I could not send the money yet. Mrs. Watkins wrote Gwyn and said she would send him something on his birthday. Gwyn went to church today and then out with some boys tonight but came in early. He plays all the time and has a gang with him all the time. Well, Darling I am tired. I went out and got breakfast for 12 people this a.m. from 10 a.m. to 1. I cooked and I am tired. I expect to sell three books tomorrow. I was down to Mr. Washington's on Friday. He bought a book and said he was so glad I brought it to him. He then took a paper and traced out our relations and he found that my grandmother Joanna Sanpre [and] his grandmother Cleo was sisters. So, *that's that*. He seemed very glad that he knew what relation we were. He complimented you wonderfully. He said his books had an awful poor sale. He then told me that John Brown's[5] only son was at his house lately and is past 70 years old.

Irma has moved to a two room apartment with her mother and they pay $9.00 per week. Too much for me. Glad you were happy over the sales I had. Will get rid of these shortly. Anita is out and has been all day. I have no where to go. Write soon. Good luck on your work.

Your,
Mom.

1. Gwyn was at this time a student at Addison Junior High School, where he did well in sports but horribly in academics.

2. A colloquial expression meaning that Homer has not been able to earn enough to buy coal with (in other words, to be useful).

3. Carrie references Dr. W. E. B. Du Bois (1868–1963), considered by many as the greatest intellectual of the twentieth century.

4. Most probably she describes James Weldon Johnson (1871–1938), a renaissance man well known for his poetry, fiction, song lyrics, and NAACP activities. He and his brother J. Rosamond Johnson wrote "Lift Every Voice," known informally as "The Negro National Anthem."

5. Brown was a God-inspired abolitionist. He led the raid on Harper's Ferry after having murdered several people in Kansas. Brown was never tried for his Kansas crimes—he was hanged rather for his crimes against the Commonwealth of Virginia.

———————

Langston Darling,

I am just waiting for you to write. But I have heard nothing. Will you please write. Now Dad has lost his job and we are all up in air to know what best to do. Homer wants to go to Kansas. I must try to get work for

I do want to send Gwyn to School another year if I can[,] so there. Now Gwyn can drive swell. He drove up to Oberlin yesterday with a crowd. Rudolph got drowned the very day his car got here and Effie[1] and Toby are nearly crazy.

Now Langston if Dad gets to Kansas, will you live with Gwyn and I this winter or what can we do. Ans this at once. Everyone here is so sad and depressed here.

Write at once

Yours
Mother.

1. Effie Burns was Carrie's cousin who lived at 2375 East 40th Street, Apartment 2525, in Cleveland, Ohio.

[Sept. 1930]
[Cleveland]

My Dearest Boy,

I was down to the old Central High School[1] today and two teachers bought books and if I had of had others I could have sold them. I sold all I had and could not fill the orders I had. So I will have to have some more. You had better send 8 more I guess, soon as you can. I have orders for five and I can sell the rest. All colored teachers I have not seen yet.

I sold Sydney Fink one and he is going to write you and he said you were the only one of Central High School class of 1920 that gave honor to the class. Also one of your old teachers said the same.

Gee, its nice to be the mother of such a nice youngster!! I tell you, your book is a seller. One of your old teachers said she'd save the book 7 years she bought until you came to autograph it for her. I had to autograph Mr. Ben Sharow book my own self as author's mother.

Now darling as I want to put a money order in this letter I have to start it off early so you can get the books off to me. We expect to move soon and get in an apartment and I will be so glad. I am so worried some times.

Gwyn went to the 8th B with flying colors, having passed the test with 92 grade. He ain't so dumb after all. Now darling, I am sending you $10.00 for I have two more books to collect from. But it's OK. You will get it next time.

Now write me at once. I am anxious at all times to hear from you.

Yours lovingly Momma

1. Central was Langston's high school alma mater, from which he graduated on June 16, 1920.

Cleveland, Ohio
September 15th [1930]

Dearest Boy,

Gwyn just got your letter and the letter from Mr. Geo. Gordon of the camp.[1] I think it was a lovely record. Don't you?

I wrote you on Thursday and enclosed $10 for sale of seven books, and I mailed it to Westfield and I was in hope you got it before you left; sorry you did not for I wanted a few more books, that I have orders for.

I owe you for two more in the last lot, and will send you what I can for it and others. I will only borrow a few dollars until Homer's work starts.

I had to buy all Gwyn's books here and I did not have quite enough money but will be all right soon. I hope your letter is sent you e're this.

On every side I hear nothing but praise of your book.

Gwyn seems fairly pleased with Cleveland. But still wishes to return to Springfield.

We want to give him a nice time on his birthday if we can.

Thanks for getting his bike, but it could have been fixed for 25¢ if he had known how.

People are in trouble straight here, no work, thousands coming in from Detroit, where all are starving. Hope you like your work.

Write

Mother

—over

You are not far from us are you? You can come over when you are through. Dad says "hello". Where in the world are you?

Dear Boy:

Here is the special sent back to me. Why did you not tell me that you were in the Hospitl? Gee you make me tired!

1. Camp Atwater was located in East Brookfield, Massachusetts. It was conducted by St. John's Institutional Activities, Inc., in Springfield, Massachusetts, for children and young adults twelve to twenty-one years old.

––––––––––

[December 1930]
Cleveland Ohio
4800 Carnegie Blvd

Dearest Boy:—I got your last letter just now. I am terrible worried. No matter what kind of engagements you have the best thing for you to do is come here to Mothers house and heal and be where I can wait on you, and take care of you fix you the right kind of food and save you your rent and expense until you are well. I can get you a good doctor here, good as there is anywhere and the best thing for you will be a quiet and rest. I will be so worried with you up there and me here and I can do more for you here than I could there for the little apartment is here. Homer thinks you should come also. Now if you have not the money to come I will try to send it to you for at home is where you could *rest* & forget everything until you were well. You have no business running around again until you are *well* [double-underlined]. I know my mother's old remedy for Tape worms, so come here & you will be cured.[1] Don't bother about Xmas. Come and get well. Now darling, mother wants you to do this for I know it is for the best. You would get well quicker. I can make you very comfortable. I will not enjoy one peaceful moment unless I come to you or you come to me and its better you come here. Cancel anything—for your health—no matter what so you can get well. I am anxious for you to come so I can fix what you can eat & to see you getting well here will relieve my terrible worry. I can't stand for you to be sick away from me. Darling come here and let me help you get well. It will be better, cheaper, & you will improve faster. For tape worms wear *one out*. Please let me hear at once what you will do. And my judgement is best this time. Don't make me wait answer at once. We don't care for Xmas. We want you well.

1. Langston did not have tapeworms. He was suffering from an inability to talk about his devastating breakup with Godmother, patron Charlotte Osgood Mason.

Cleveland Ohio

Sunday P.M.

Dear Langston

I was here thinking of everything and I wish I was coming to N.Y. for Xmas to see you but it is out of the question for I have no job and we pay $44.00 per month rent, and If Homer was not making pretty good we could not make those expenses. But when you come will see you. Say here in Cleveland Antiques are all the rage and I was just wondering if we could not sell the Harper's Ferry Shawl? I almost know we could and it would give us all a few dollars. Do you know where it is or do you have a receipt or anything for it. A man told me here last week I ought to get $500.00 for it. I have been in some of the antique shops here and they have old rugs, spreads, quilts &ct. I don't know just thought I'd ask about it.

We have a Victrola and I have been playing "Moaning Low" this morning and Gwyn says "My goodness why play one piece all the time." But I know that is one of your favorites.

Homer says he is getting us all a radio for Xmas. Says that will be the Xmas present for all. Gwyn was very proud last night, his first pay day. He is delivering after school, at the White Y.M.C.A. Tailor Shop and with tips and all he made $5.00 and over. He bought me a pair hose and Dad a shirt. Said he had to get you & Uncle Stokins a present also.

Well, I do hope you are better. I worried so about you being sick away from me. Of course, I can't realize you are grown and don't need mother any more. But I'd like to be near you when you are ill. I can't help it.

We were out to Amelie's[1] last night until 1 A.M. listening over the radio at Gene and Glenn giving the program for the poor children Xmas fund. Cleveland has raised over an enourmous fund. Seems no one here need be hungry or cold or without Xmas presents.

I have no money to buy Xmas presents so will send cards. Is Helen at the same place? Is Toy's number 2 E 127th?[2] Also send me Mrs. Thompson's address. Want to send them a card, and our cousins. How is Hall and every one? Old lady McDonald says if you have to tape worm, she can cure it in no time. Says she has brought many one away.

Well I guess I will stop now. I wanted to go to church today but have no heavy coat so I had to stay in. My old fur coat fell to piece entirely, but I am going to try to get one after Xmas. It snowed here some today and rained and it is not cold. Amelie sends her love and says she hope you are much better. Do you remember Pet? She comes often and asks about you and she is still waiting to marry you. Now answer at once. Let me know how you are. Don't try to buy any Xmas presents for us. Times are to tight. Get well. Come back down here and rest. See no one rest, sleep and eat. —Yours lovingly Mother.

1. Amelia McNaughton was Carrie's cousin. Carrie spelled Amelia's name variously, including "Amele" and "Amelie." This relative gave Langston a fountain pen for his high school graduation; he carried it with him around the world for twenty-five years. It is a part of his collection at the Beinecke Library at Yale University.

2. Ethel "Toy" Harper was a longtime friend of Carrie's from Garnett, Kansas. A tiny, doll-like woman, Toy left Kansas at age fifteen to join a medicine show. Toy performed as a snake charmer and in various other roles. With many talents, she performed in plays, and her enactment of Langston's poem "The Negro Mother" earned her high praise. She also volunteered her time as a seamstress and looked out for Langston and his interests when he was not in New York. Langston would move into the New York apartment of Toy and her musician husband, Emerson, at 634 St. Nicholas Avenue, in 1942. In 1947 the three of them would move into a house at 20 East 127th Street in Harlem. Langston would live there for the rest of his life. He willed his interest in the home to Toy, with the stipulation that if she died before her husband, Emerson could live in the house rent-free for the rest of his life.

Oberlin, Ohio
58 E. Vine St.
[March 1931]

Dear Langston,

I just got your letter. I am sending you the marriage certificate and tell you the Drs. Name was Dr. Long of New York City, who had then just came to Joplin and was with old Dr. Aubach, who was our Doctor. Now maybe that with these [you can get] the birth certificate. For they did have them then 1902.

Gwyn is better and setting up and trying to get ready to go to a Basket Ball game on Sat. night. He is so silly. I hope things will get better now. If it only gets warmer.

I will write more again but want to get this off. I am hungry. I worked two hours this A.M. got 35¢ and that looked fine to me. Ha! Ha!

Write and do get through and come away from there.

Mamma

———————

Cleveland Ohio
March 31st [1931]

Dearest Boy in the world:—I wrote you at the Crisis[1] and now since I got your card to Gwyn I write you again. And will sent it air mail so you will get this quick.

I had thought of you so much and hoped you got over to New York and back all safe and sound and so glad to get your card and see you were all O.K. You are the Dearest Boy in the world and to know you are my own Boy, my very own—Oh! You were so lovely to me on the western trip. I hesitated about coming out for fear you might not be so glad but it made me so happy when you were glad to see me. And you were so lovely. I can never never forget that visit. I was so happy.

Everything so lovely.

I got the papers, thanks so much. I liked the write ups. There were all very nice. I think on the whole your trip was very lovely. Don't you? Say please send me Mr. Lewis (Raddie) address, also Mrs. Dr. Radbury, the woman I stopped with in K.C. want to write to her a card of thanks. Also to say a few words to her Mother. Dearest I hope you will be home this summer. Gwyn wants a job very much this summer. He don't know what He wants to do. He's got lots of plans, but wants to hear from you. I hope you will have a nice time in Texas & California.

Be careful in Texas for it's the worst in the Union.

Write when you can. If you have time send a card of sympathy to Mrs. Alberta Hunter,[2] who lost her husband. Her address is 7501 Cedar St. Now dearest I am stopping for know you won't have much time to read.

Who did you see in N.Y. Did you see Irene.

Your loving Mother
C. M. Clark

1. Subtitled *A Record of the Darker Races*, the monthly magazine of the NAACP, *The Crisis*, was founded by W. E. B. Du Bois.

2. A renowned New York performer, Hunter (1895–1984) achieved fame as a blues and jazz singer beginning in the 1920s. Critics often favorably compared her to such popular performers as Ethel Waters and Bessie Smith.

Cleveland Ohio
Sept. 13th [1931]

My Dear Boy:—Your letter rec'd and was very glad as I am always to hear from you. You are a very sweet boy to write me so often now.

Yes, the whole of "Scarlet Sister Mary"[1] was a "flop." Every one was disgusted at the whole thing here.

The Whitmans were here this week and as usual had a good show and crowded house.

I could not find the article in the Defender. Send the clipping to me I will return it to you.

Cecil is trying hard to get a concert here. May be he will next month.

Dad, who is famous for saying he will write, just said, well "I'll get Langstons address and write him a letter." I said yes? For I know that is the end of it.

Gwyn is all right but does not obey me at all, stays out every night until 10 Bells. I have talked, talked, and all to no avail. So we just have to go on. I can't do one thing but hope for the best.

I don't see what to say to the Dr. Rev. Brown, or to the High School, either for they both feel if you come here you must appear in their place. Of course you are "scared of lots of people" for its not a very happy situation before a large crowd and they all expect you to entertain them.

Well enclosed find $5.00 these books are not going so fast.

Write

Your Mother.

Baby Boy,

You can sure get a crowd here and make some money. When are you coming East? I want you to be sure to stop and see us if you can come soon. We all just crazy to see you. It has been so long since I saw my only Dear Son. I am just so anxious to see you. Where will Mr. Hayes sing? And will you get a pull off it. All the others Do. For I know that is the way Louise and Patterson made their living and they did live well. It is all a graft. Now everyone is trying to get money—Scottsboro boys! and most all of it the poor boys don't even get a "smell." But I don't believe anything will get them out now but God and he will have to destroy every jail in Ala.

1. Carrie refers here to the play based on the novel about Gullah life written by Julia Peterkin, a White South Carolinian. It opened originally on September 26, 1930, at the Hartman Theatre in Columbus, Ohio.

———————

Cleveland Ohio
Nov. 17th [1931]

My Dearest Boy:—

Your letter came to me today and I was so anxious to hear. And oh my dearest dear, you are doing just wonderful. That clipping is so very fine and I am so proud of my own boy. You are a Darling. But you can only be with you. Can't you take off part of your tour? The Youngs in Buffalo, Mr. Mason said the Club wants me to come there, so they can meet your mother. He spent a whole after noon with me. Langston it is so lovely to be known as your mother. For you are wonderful. Cousin Julia is here with us now. She says tell you that she loves you and is so proud of you she sends you hundreds kisses.

Gwyn the rascal, is very important in foot ball and Basket Ball,[1] and he sent me the money. I got him and a suit [*sic*] and have nothing for my self. He has to look nice at school. He has new shoes to last Saturday. Now I told him I was going to try to get something for myself.

Langston when will you be here? Everyone hopes you come here this spring. The clubs want you so bad. Also Methodist church and "Noon Day Club" and several others. I sold two books and have money. I will send the money to you. So please write me as only you can. Homer has not been here since Oct 1st and its been lonely here as summer, some days its 74. Its grand weather and I have not had to have any heat. We have a nice view now. I wish you could see what its like and then you will come on home some day. When will I get the promised ride in the car? It is another 4 day excursion to New York, Nov 25th. I have not seen him up since last summer. I hope you will go to Kansas for Auntie Reed wrote me such a sad letter when Dess [Desalines Langston] passed and she wants to hear from you. Write her when you can. The old Lawrence Journal[2] had a nice piece about him and you being his nephew. Darling I am overloaded you now. Things are getting very bad. I have to get with glasses very bad. One eye is all swelled up. I am so sorry you can't be here no time soon. Not even Xmas.

Much love and Kisses
Mother

Mel says hello says tell us when you go to Florida.

---

1. Gwyn enrolled in Central High School in Cleveland, Ohio, after leaving school in Springfield, Massachusetts.

2. The *Lawrence Journal-World* was—and still is—the largest newspaper in Lawrence, Kansas.

———————

Cleveland, Ohio
Friday
[Dec. 11, 1931]

Darling, my own Boy,

Oh, I just got your message and so glad you are all right and happy.

But I am so worried about you. I can not eat nor sleep hardly and I am so nervous that I am nearly sick. I can not stand the worry. They have all got me scared about your going to Alabama. Rev Southerland has got some literature from there and he has got people all up in arms and I was not so worried until he came out and he asked me how I could be so calm and you in danger. He is having you prayed for at the altar and so you see how the people feel up here. Please darling, if you love me don't go through Alabama for they say feelings there is terrible against the Northerns now and if I know you are there I can't stand it. Please. Please *don't go* ["go" is double-underlined]. Cancel this engagement for your life is worth more than every dollar in the world. Now don't be hard headed. Father Southerland says the Cointelpro[1] was sent down to Scottsboro. Please don't go.

We are all well but Gwyn and Homer and I are all so worried about you. Oh I wish you could come home for one day any way at Xmas. Couldn't you drive up here in two days. I do want to see you so bad. And you must be careful for Homer says those people are so treacherous, you can never tell how they feel, you cannot trust them, so now please listen, for I would just give up if something happened to you.

Answer this at once. Julia stays with us for she was outdoors and I took her in. Oh! I want you to come home. Write me at once.

Your loving mother

1. "COINTELPRO" stood for Counter Intelligence Program, a domestic spying program of the Federal Bureau of Investigation.

———————

Last payment car due Oct. 14th

Saw Cora Wallace in Topeka. Just as mad as a "hatter." Writing a novel. Says it will be great. Wants your help. Would you write her

Cleveland, Ohio

Sept. 19, 1932

My Dear Son—

It is certainly a relief to write to you. All the newspapers here has had me all upset and I did not know where you were or what and I have been so worried that I did not have the heart to write any one.

We went to Kansas July 13th and stayed four weeks. Mrs. Clarke[1] was so ill we came away, left Homer there and stayed one week with Mae Perkins who just lost her father. When we got back I expected sure to get a job, but as yet I have nothing. Gwyn could get nothing, so here we have been. So worried, so heart sick, I've done every way to get along, have not as yet got any books for Gwyn but will now from this check. This is the worse depression U.S. ever had, people are just committing suicide for fun. We just got in, passed a house on 89th where the police was bringing out a woman, who committed. She just lost her home—so died—The charities are over crowded, plenty foreigners who can't even speak English—crowding to get food. The law cannot make any one pay rent and all the teachers have not been paid, part still owed for last year. Pet went back to school to teach with the promise she would get paid. Few can pay their taxes therefore all city jobs do not pay. People are paying $3.00 per week, some $2.00 some 50¢ per day. Any only a few can get that. So Darling, if you can pay to eat and sleep there it is good, for thousands here are out doors. I told Gwyn that he and I would go out in the car and stay if something did not happen soon. Many families are out in the cars begging a little to eat. Langston you should have written before. I needed you to write. I am glad you told me the truth of the picture as it was in colored papers that some of you were sick and could not leave Russia.[2] That none of the contracts would be filled and you all could not come back to U.S.

I'd like to see "Dream Keeper"[3] have not yet see a copy and hope to see "Popo and Fifina."[4]

Gwyn started to school today. He came back so tired, he is not so strong and eats very little. He has been worried terrible because he feared he could not go to school, but I hope he can. No, after Homer lost his job we did not take $15.00 to send Gwyn to summer school, because that was all we had until some one got work, as yet none of us have made nothing.

The car is just great. I am so happy to have (over) it, and oh Can I come to Russia? how Gwyn and I have enjoyed it as long as we could buy gas we rode around trying to get work, trying to "tote" people places ect [etc.]. And make a little money, but nothing doing. The car runs lovely, we have had it lubricated last month, it is ok. Gwyn says it needs one brake lined, but I can't do it just now, for about a month we could buy one gal gas, go to employment offices for that was much cheaper than car fare. Gwyn drives wonderful but could not get drivers license until after his birthday Sept. 24th. If I don't get work we will have to drive to Russia. If I can get some one to keep Gwyn, I will go try N.Y. maybe. Did I tell you that Rudolph got drowned. Poor Effie. It was a sad blow to her. Amelie just the same. Had no work at all. We have had some very good offers for the car but no sell. I rather have the car than anything I ever had, so I can't let it ever go. I tried to ascertain about the insurance and I think it's due also Oct. I don't see the date on the papers. I will save all paper clippings I see for you. I'd love to be there with you. Give my regards to Louise.[5] Who is that with you in the picture? Green pastures[6] will be here very soon. Aunt Sallie[7] is very chummie with your father. He may come up to her (funny).

1. Homer's mother lived in Topeka, Kansas. Carrie variously spelled her last name with and without the ending "e."

2. In June 1932, Langston sailed with twenty-one other African Americans to the Soviet Union, where they had been commissioned to make a communist-inspired film about race relations in the United States. Louise Thompson had coordinated the effort, which ultimately failed. The film, to have been titled *Black and White*, was never made. After the collapse of the project, Langston remained in the Soviet Union for a year.

3. A selection of Hughes's poems for young people published by Knopf.

4. A children's book coauthored with Arna Bontemps and published by Macmillan, 1932.

5. Louise Thompson.

6. An all-Black play, *Green Pastures* opened on February 26, 1930, to rave reviews by Broadway critics and audiences. The principal character in the religious fantasy, "De Lawd," was played by Richard B. Harrison, a former Pullman porter.

7. James N. Hughes's sister, Sallie Garvin, lived in Indianapolis, Indiana.

New York, N.Y.

Feb 15th [1933]

Mr. Dearest Boy,

So glad to get your letter. For it has been so long since I had a letter and after all I do want something beside the cablegrams (sometime), But they are lovely anyway. I do hope you are all o.k. and that you can get your passport renewed so that you will start home at the first start of spring. Yes, your mother is an actress at last, the dream I dreamed as a little child is very near realized. I *am* one of the principals in Hall Johnson's show "Run Little Chillun Run." Hall himself wrote the show and it is a discussion between two churches or rather the Hope Baptist Church of Charlestown.[1]

Hall wrote the show and all the music the African music is beautiful. Yes he is back. He is very high since he returned, over coats and suits galore very high class. He is all to grand for me. The choir made the tour in a bus.

Aunt Sallie hears from your father now she said.[2] Hope her nerves are easy. She worried until she heard. Here is a little slip about the show all I can find just now. But the play is marvelous and I hope it goes over big. If I can get about 6 months all I need. Ha! Ha! Helen is fine same job, same money, same hateful little black gal, and she hit the numbers yesterday. I can't stand her nor Blanch any more they have wished all sorts of bad luck on the play because Blanch got mad and quit it. Now they hope it's no good. *Pure Niggers.*

Freddie Washington,[3] Austin Burleigh, Edna Thomas, Lillie King, De-Witt Spencer and I!!! Are the principals. And the African New Day Pilgrims. A Negro cult—I think [you] ought to be over here for the opening.

Will you stay in Japan or China long? I have two good spots in the show. I am going to try to get some clippings from the press tomorrow for you. I will send them to you.

As yet I have no money and poor little Gwyn is moneyless and I don't know how he gets on. I could not get work, so just rehearsed and rehearsed now in two weeks we will go to work. Send me some money if you ever get the book money or if you have any. Roosevelt [the] New Pres[ident] was already shot at and Mayor of Chicago killed—or at least can't live.[4]

Louise's mother[5] is expected to pass any minute. I am there now. Louise also is very ill. Wallie is crazy. Don't fool with him for he may hurt you. He is very jealous of you and Louise.

Mr. Rockmore, Mr. Frank Martin, Mr. Simons, all know you well. They are buyers and directors.

Emmerson[6] is still in Rhapsody in Black[7] but making no money. Toy is quite busy. I do not pay her any room rent, but work all the time I can to keep her house clean and get her meals. Ruby[8] of Scottsboro fame wrote a letter which exonerated the boys but they are still held.

Dad is crazy. I do not know what he will do. He just stays out there and does not send us a thing nor write. I am sick of everything so I don't bother.

Louise has been working and speaking until she has worn herself out and no revolutions yet. Ha! Ha! I want her to wait until the show goes on. I am afraid I can't sell the car as I have no money to get it to New York even. And then I do not know what conditions it is in since Gwyn had the accident. Gwyn passed in all his work this term even if he hadn't the first cent. I expect he is flat bare footed.

Write me at once

Yours *Mother*.

1. The play is concerned with the conflict between the Christian and African religious heritage in Black life.

2. Sallie Garvin wrote her brother James on December 22, 1932, that Carrie told her she had not heard from Langston for seven weeks. Sallie wrote that she was "afraid he is not as thoughtful of the future as he should be. He is like his mother when it comes to spending money. The kind of life he leads seems to be characteristic of all literary people they are all great spenders and like high life. With this opportunity to travel someday he will make a great writer."

3. Fredi Washington was a beautiful, successful cabaret singer who played the role of Sulamai in the play. Aston Burleigh played the role of Jim, the pastor's son who was tempted by Sulamai. Edna Thomas was listed by James Weldon Johnson as one of the notable performers at the Lincoln and Lafayette Theaters.

4. On the evening of February 15, 1933, before he had taken the oath of office, President-elect Roosevelt, just back from a yachting trip to the Bahamas, was in Miami, sitting in the back of his car after making a short speech to twenty thousand or so people, when a man named Giuseppe Zangara fired five quick shots at him. After the first shot, a nearby specta-

tor, Lillian Cross, grabbed the gunman's arm and saved Roosevelt's life. Anton J. Cermak died weeks later from his gunshot wounds.

5. She refers here to Louise Thompson. "Wallie" is Wallace Thurman, Louise's husband. Thurman was later to marry again without having divorced Louise. Known to be a homosexual, Thurman never spoke of his sexual practices to Louise. Zora Neale Hurston was also very jealous of the relationship between Louise and Langston. Louise's claim that Langston was asexual was never believed by either Hurston or Thurman.

6. She refers here to Emerson Harper.

7. The reference is to a popular Black musical of the era.

8. Ruby Bates was one of the White women the Scottsboro Boys were accused of raping; the other was Victoria Price.

SPECIAL
Program of Margaret Bonds, Pianist and John Greene, Baritone, at the Abraham Lincoln Center 700 Oakwood Boulevard. Three of Hughes's librettos, "Poeme d'Automne," "Sylvester's Dying Bed," and "Midnight Nan," were being performed.

New York, N.Y.
March 22, 1933

Mr. Dear Boy—

Just got your letter and I was so glad to hear. The show is wonderful. Gloria Swanson,[1] Carl Van Vechten, Charlie Chaplin,[2] Lillian Dittmer, Norman [Norma] Shearer, Edgar [Edward G.] Robinson. And numerous others have been to show and pronounced it marvelous. The critics are very enthusiastic and say they believe the play will last a year here.

As you say, it will be a miracle if it runs with all broke. As the show opened the banks closed. Every thing seemed against us but we are fighting on with a cast of 175, and the cast was cut today to 125 plenty.

Oh! I first heard that Junita Lewis[3] came today. I will try to see her and see what she says about you.

When are you coming home?

The Herald Tribune, The News, The World Telegram, The Sun, All have had wonderful write ups. Toy and Emerson are well. Have the Harpers Leonard and Arsie in there home.

Did you ever see such paper? Bought it on the way to Theater. So don't think I am going back. I know better. Hope you get here to see the show. Every time there is a celebrity in the audience. Mr. Simons announces it to us, so I told him to announce it when you were in the audience Ha! Ha! Well, I can send you to some clippings but you may be here.

Thanks for money. Your Mother Carolyn.

1. Gloria Swanson (1899–1983) was an Academy Award–nominated, Golden Globe–winning American Hollywood actress who was especially prolific during the silent film era.

2. Charlie Chaplin was a pioneer in the world of cinema and a founder of United Artists. His Little Tramp was perhaps the best-known character of the silent film era.

3. Juanita Lewis was a professional singer who sang with Hall Johnson's choir.

New York, N.Y.
May 13th [*sic*] [1933]

My Dearest Boy:

Thanks awfully for the card also for the letter. I love to hear from you, but I realize you are busy and don't have time to write, but you love me just the same don't you? And today being Mother's day you don't love any one better do you? Langston, I bet you smile and say "Mother is getting old and simple." I was at Metropolitan Church this P.M. and the program was very nice. Of course, Mothers were lauded and relauded. Poor things so many true and untrue things said of some. I have a piece on the Victrola belonging to Mrs. Thomas that I heard before I ever heard of you, and the memories it brings back. We used to dance by it in Hot Springs Ark. When I was 14 yrs old. And you know that was along time ago, and there was my first love affair and I was immediately sent home. For my aunt, dear old soul, thought I might run off and marry and I might. So back home I went with the reputation I was head strong and impudent!! So that ended a very pleasant visit of long ago.

Now tell me your first love affair. Fair exchange of stories eh?

Did you see Zora's article in the Pittsburgh Courier? Very good. I like it. Wish I had kept some of her letters. They were very sweet.

Yes, Langston I did enjoy little old Gwyn, but some way he is older and seems to be out growing me also. Of course you were always grown beyond my reach, but Gwyn has been my baby so long I hate to give him up to be a grown fellow. He does look better but he was not so well. He had a very bad cold. He is so tall. So way up in the air. But he's a darling just the same. Langston, today made me wonder have I been all a Mother could be to you & Gwyn. I mean a poor Mother? Does it seem to you that I have been all the name implies, some time I feel that you & I were never as close. Heart & heart as we should be, but I have loved you very dearly and if I failed in some things it was lack of knowledge.

It is very cold here and I am so sorry Gwyn left his coat here. I know he needs it. Poor little fellow. He did not want to go back, he said he did not like up there but he's all right. Write when you can. Did you enjoy Hampton?[1]

Yours Mother.

1. Hampton Institute is a historically Black college in Hampton, Virginia.

———————

N.Y. N.Y. [1933]
Sunday night

Well Dearest:—

It's raining but guess what I have done this P.M.? Went down to the civic club all alone to hear Mrs. Georgia Douglas Johnson, and I was so glad I went for I had a lovely time. One of the White ladies of the Penguin Club of Washington was over and she knew me and between she and Mr. Dill, Mrs. Douglas Johnson [and] I had a good time.[1]

Every one asked for you. Dr. DuBois was there, the bride is in bed with the gripp.

Mrs. Johnson read very very well. I like her style. She read the one you, Bruce, Alexander &ct said was the best one they every wrote and it was the list of titles of her books.[2] Wasn't that funny. Do you remember?

I wrote Gwyn, only got a short note he said he had been sick for a few days. I will send the $1.00 this week for him.

I am up to Dr. Savory for a few weeks. She has been very very sick. I will only be there a short time I think. I am very very sleepy I can't seem to stay awake. You can buy plenty jobs here. But can not pick up many. Talked for some time with Mr. Dill this afternoon. He seems very fond of you. He asked me when [you] would be in town again.

Langston where is Zora and when will she be back in New York? Let me know.

Is Sartar here yet?

To bad you won't be up for so long. Some one at the Civic Club today said you must come back there and read. It was nice so informal. Every one so pleasant.

Write when you can   Will be glad to see either.

Yours truly,
M

1. Augustus Granville Dill was the business manager of *The Crisis*.
2. Here she references Richard Bruce Nugent.

Cleveland, Ohio
Aug 22 [1933]
2245 E 80th

My Dear Langston

I was so happy to hear you this A.M. I am just so very happy now, and I came back to bed and proceeded to write you at once. I am sad to have to write you at this time like this but I am just at the jumping off place and no work and no money at all. I am for the first time in my life with no where to go. No place to stay, no job and no money. I rehearsed with the show. I played with it, and I made no money, wasted time but there was no work anyway. I could get nothing to do. I worked for my room and board at Toy's for month and was nearly worked to death. Then she got peeved and I left and then play[ed] the show on promises, five months and two weeks. I got behind with Gwyn. I got behind with everything, then when the show closed I had to go back to Toy's and finally I got very ill and was sick one month and the charities through the Urban League in New York send me to Cousin Lucy where Gwyn is, in Oberlin. I was there four weeks, and I got some better, but far from well now, and Amele got very ill and they sent for me to take care of her. So again I'm here for room and board nearly worked to death. I am not well yet myself. But what can I do. I owe Cousin Lucy for Gwyn. She's old. Her and cousin John but they have been wonderful to both of us. Oh! They are so kind. When I ever get anything again I will remember them. Gwyn had a wreck with them on New Year's Eve and came with in an inch of getting killed broke up the car. I had to get a liscense from the dealer in N.Y. to bring it there, and he gave me $75, and $50.00 deposit on . . . another one. Of course the deposit is there yet. I put a suit of clothes and shoes on Gwyn and paid Cousin Lucy $25 for Gwyn's board. Of course I had nothing, then I was so sick I could hardly walk.

Homer was very low. I don't know how he is. His mother left the home and none of them can pay the taxes and he wanted me to buy it in but with what? But as soon as you can I must have a place to live. I could get a nice little place cheap in Oberlin. I love it there. Write me very soon.

I hate to write you this kind of letter but Langston I don't know what to do. Gwyn wants to stay in Oberlin. I have no money to do any thing at all but if I could rent a little house then we could stay and now as things are getting better may be I could get work and Gwyn get some work and we could make it. If I could get work I would not ask any one. But I have been so poorly and being so worried I have nearly died. OH! Worry will kill any one. I hope thing will get better now. I will be here another week then back to Oberlin and I don't know what there. My insurance is yours & Gwyn's needs paying now.

Write me a long letter and tell me what you suggest. I am getting old and I have to do something now, so I won't always be out doors. Oh!

Langston I am so glad you are back in the states. Can't you come settle and make a home or help to for us. I need you so much now. I can't stand this knocking around much more. Please write me a nice comforting letter.

Yours truly,

Mamma.

[September 1933]

Sunday

Darling Boy:—so sorry to write you such a disturbing letter. I saw no way out and I was so discouraged. Dad has been terribly ill. I have had no work since the show closed. Gwyn has had none, so you see I did not know what to do or which way to turn. Now things do look brighter that I may at least get work. If I could only be assured of a place to live could get along. Rent so cheap in Oberlin, but I can see no work there. Cleveland I may be able to get work. I don't know yet, but then there is Gwyn. But Oh!! I pray times will be better now. But Langston you don't know it has been terrible. I have just been worried to death nearly. I have worked for room and board until I'm heart sick. I want work I don't want charity at all. Amele had an operation and has been to the hospital and I am here doing the work for she and Pet. Amele has been sick some time so has no money and the teachers have not been paid for Lord knows "when" when she has very little. I hope to be away from here soon. I hate to leave her helpless for someday they will have something and will remember me. Gwyn came up from Oberlin tonight with some boys, and he wants to know if you need some one to drive you on [your] lecture tour. He is here to get shoes and he wants a sweater for his birthday.

I just got a letter from one of the boys in the show and he tells me that he is afraid the choir is badly shattered, as over to the Stadium at Philly Hall[1] was drunk and that he called the head members of the choir "god-damn liars" and then said they were "lousy" so they all struck and one of them lamed Hall across the head, so I fear the choir is no more. To bad. Well I hope that they will make it up for they are to good to fall down like that. Hall was getting so very grand and unbearable when I left there. But nice to me.

Well, Langston, there is no use telling you how thankful I am for I can't never tell you that I am so sorry I ever have to bother you at all. But what can I do. I wish you could get work for Gwyn some where. He is smart to work and likes it, but can get nothing at all to do. He needs to learn now to help himself some. I will do all I can to get work somewhere. I am much better than I was. I was very very ill could not hardly make it at all. But I am better oh! How much I want to see you. I am just sick to see you but I know how you feel about coming east.

Write and thousand thanks & kisses
From
Mamma

1. She refers to Hall Johnson here.

———————

[September 1933]
Oberlin Ohio
215 S Park St

My Dear Son: Very glad to hear from you. Also glad you wrote Gwyn. But you seem to have misunderstood my attitude as to Gwyn going to school. For you say "you hope I will *let* [double-underlined] Gwyn go to school and encourage him." Why did I work my self nearly to deth always—but to see him in School. Last winter I would often been hungry, if it had not been for kindness of friends. All I had, or could make, Gwyn got to try to keep him through the winter. When Spring came, I owed Cousin Lucy three months board and room, then I got sick, could not work, she kindly offered to take me to her house until I was better, so I have been here most of the time, as yet have been unable to get work. The Urban League[1] sent to the Welfare Board. They paid my way here.

What did I have when we talked of school, to encourage Gwyn to keep on. I had no where to stay. I could pay nothing for him. I could not even

To Jessica Hudgins

1011 County Line Trail

Maysfield, GA 30055

United States 即美國

Dear Jessica (洪潔西)
There is a tree in the post card.
I am struggling holding this pen.
As you know, I have never written
a postcard. So I don't know
what to write. But I bet this
would be fun surprise to see Priscilla
ah much better. I am glad you
agreed to eat at Mcdonalds.!
I hope that as the day goes on
you will be in a better mood
on account of forgetting your
blisters because you ate with
your good friend Priscilla.
Thanks,

阿里山神木
阿里山神木於1998年6月放倒於神木車站供人觀賞

ask Aunt Lucy to keep him as I was in debt to her and no work & no money. She & Cousin John are quite old have a home here, but don't work and I can't impose on them any more. So I had nothing to offer for encouragement for my self let alone Gwyn. I told him if I got work I would keep him an send him to school when you have sent me the money. I saw Cousin Lucy and Cousin John refused flatly to keep him. So Gwyn felt so terrible over it he wrote you and when your letter came, we tried again to get the cousins to consent after you assured them of this where with[al]. But "no" Cousin Lucy up in terrible poor health and just don't feel she can, and I guess Cousin John feels he would like all back pay and not start more. But now you see, I hope. I had nothing to promise. Now Gwyn and I see that he can stay if you are willing, by getting a small house, and both of us trying to get something. I put an ad in the paper today. Gwyn went to see the foot ball coach, see if he would help him get something. I'd do any way to keep him here, but no one here will board him only with terrible expense and both of us could live for what he could. If you think that is good idea we will try it. Dad is very ill.[2] He has no work had to depend on his sister & brother for food himself. Their house will be sold for taxes soon.

I could not go out there and starve rather go from Cleveland to the poor farm at Warrensville. This living matter now is terrible, I tell you. I can get a swell house here for $10.00. Other expenses will be about 8 or 10 that is cheaper than you could pay board for Gwyn. I have a cousin here with a truck, says he will bring what things I have in Cleveland over here. I will only have to buy a few things. If you want me to do this I will do it for Gwyn's sake, I can't show encouragement in a better way.

So answer at once, for we have to get some where at once. They only have one spare room and they want it. So we have to go some where. Sorry you feel I *don't* want Gwyn to finish. I do and sorry I can't do for him.

—M

"Run Little Chillun" seems to have run out. One of the members wrote me that the choir had all severed it connection with Hall, and he cussed them out and told them he was through with them for ever. I would not go back to them with out another contract and back money. They owe us all so much.

I liked your story in the American Mercury: It was very good. Have not seen a Scribner yet.[3]

Please answer us at once as Gwyn is so worried he is sick today and gone to bed, poor boy. He's had it tough enough this past year.

There's nothing else to say I don't believe.

1. In response to Harlem's rapid growth, the National Urban League began as a national organization to help provide temporary housing, child care, and job counseling to Black migrants. It also tackled issues of working-class city dwellers, including negotiations with public officials, police, landlords, and employers.

2. Homer was then living in Topeka, Kansas, with family.

3. "Cora Unashamed" appeared in *American Mercury* (September 1933), and "Slave on the Black" in *Scribner's Magazine* (September 1933).

Oberlin Ohio

215 S Park

My Dear Boy:—

I just got your card also the box. The things are wonderful. I am just very please with the beads and cigarette holder. Gwyn and I have already argued over the holder, he says it was his and I say it is mine.

Gwyn started to school Monday and I told him no fooling, he must apply him self to his books this year. As yet I have no work. I have advertised, I've walked. I mean to do all possible to get a job. NRA means very little over this way, as yet very few colored people have been benefited.

I am willing to get out and fight for work. If it would do any good. As yet have not heard a word from Dad do not know whether he is dead or not. I felt so sorry about him but could do not one thing. I hold not a cent either.

Cousin Erma is very ill. But I don't know where they live so don't know how she is now.

The Freshmans at the College are having their celebration on the campus tonight. So Gwyn has gone out first time this week. He is playing foot Ball getting—

I wrote Toy tonight to see if she would send me my coat I left in N.Y.

Have not heard any thing about "Run Little Chillun." Did you write us last week if so it got lost in the Air Mail. As the Pilot was lost for days in a swamp.

Write soon—

Mamma

[September 17, 1933]

Oberlin, Ohio

Dear Son,

We have moved and as yet have no gas but will get along ok until we can get it.

I am so glad to be in these rooms for I have taken slurs and been made to feel terrible, until any place is a haven. I am paying $10.00, then will have gas and lights, if not too high. If so I can burn coal and oil lamps. Langston I walked everywhere yesterday trying to find a job but as yet have none. Gwyn got to wash a car today.

First there is one favor I want to ask you. George Freeman, a distant cousin, made it possible for us to do all we did. He moved us for only gas for his truck, went to Cleveland and got what I had. Gave me everything else he had, then gave me potatoes and other vegetables. Now he's gone to try to get gas for us. He is 63 years old, lives in a shack here (is contrary, very odd, very wicked, very proud of all you do, talks of you to everyone as *his* cousin), but he has been a *prince* to Gwyn and I. Now I want you to write him a letter and send to him. He will be the proudest person in the world. Just thank him for us all. He won't let me even say "thanks." *Do this* [double-underlined]. This letter came from Bessie's so I opened it to see if was worth sending you and so I just put it in mine.

Gwyn is so pleased that he could stay here. He is anxious to get work and go to School. I paid first month's rent, got what things I had to have to live up here. Now am getting some eats. Try to last until next month. The next rent will be due Oct. 12th. Gwyn worked today will get most of his books.

If you could come here and stay with us and write and be quiet for months. No one here to bother any one. If I get work. You come here and stay.

Have not heard a word from Dad further don't know how he got.

Now I will be looking for a letter soon. I went up to the Library and read your story in Scribners. It sure was good. I am trying a short story for the news. $5.00 if one wins.

Oh! I want work so bad but don't know what to do. Well dear write. Did you write Mr. Hughes.[1] Sallie said he wanted you to.

Mother

1. A reference to Langston's father.

[October 1933]
Sunday
Oberlin, Ohio
117 S. Main St.

My Dearest Boy,

I just got your letter this eve. A man was up to the post office, he's our carrier. Came by and brought it. Also a letter from New York, announcing the opening of "Run Little Children" in Boston Nov. 10th. Today, I got my first days work. I got to work extra. I was very glad. Hope I can get some regular work. I have been doing a little. I take in sewing when I can get it, work may be an hour or so but as yet can't get much and they pay so little.

Gwyn has a Sunday morning paper route for a while also. He gets a little off of that. He and I live just as cheap as we can. I am getting along in the house very well. I will have to get a small coal stove and burn as gas is too high here to heat with. But Cousin Lucy has given us a oil stove that does fine now. Every one of the relatives are lovely to us and are all wanting *you* for dinner Thanksgiving. Oberlin people are very proud of you.

Yes, the check was here on time rent is due on Wednesday and Gas and light tomorrow. Oh! I cannot tell you how I thank you and if I can get work,—You won't have to do so much. I am praying every day for a job.

I will get one some time I know. I am pretty tired tonight so I won't write much. I will write more later. Will tell you how the bills were. Yes, do write to cousin George. You can send it to me or to Grovenor St. George Freeman, anyone here knows him. He is a character. Came over Saturday said, "have you plenty to eat. I have good credit." He is funny. Makes all kinds of liquor and *drinks none*. Treats all friends.

Yours,
Mother.

Oct. 9th 1933

My Dear Mrs. Hughes-Clark

Mr. Rockmore is going to take the show on a tour with plans to open in Boston Nov. 7th or 13th if you will be interested in going at $25.00 a week let me know immediately may be able to get you $30.00 if you wish to do the same Hunt sister part.

Very truly Yours,
J. De Witt Spencer
9 East 131 St
New York, NY

Oct. 12/33

My Dear Miss Clark

Received your letter we are starting rehearsals Oct. 16th will you try and get here not later than the 23rd. we are rehearsing at 229 Lenox Ave.

Very Truly,
J. De Witt Spencer

Dear Boy,

My own angel son. Just saw your last story in Mercury.[1] Oh! It's grand. I *love it*. Enclosed find letters about the show. So just keep them. May need. Now, I get a message to be there the 30th instead. We will get $25.00 according to N.R.A.[2] Mr. Ricknieve says he can't pay less. $5.00 bonus. So would you go? I will send for Dad let him take care of Gwyn. We expect to stay out 10 weeks. (over)

I would like to try it out once more if I do no good the house and Gwyn will still be here. What do you say? If I make good you will be helped so you won't have to strain to make ends meet. But I want to keep my home here.

Oh! I hope you can see the show this time. Try hard won't you?

Answer by return as I have to leave Friday Eve. Telegraph if no other way. 117 S. Maine St. Carolyn

1. *American Mercury*. She refers to "Poor Little Black Fellow" (November 1933).

2. The production of *Run, Little Chillun* was funded in part by the National Recovery Administration. The NRA was a federal agency created under the National Industrial Recovery Act of June 16, 1933, and abolished on January 1, 1936, after the law's major provisions were held to be unconstitutional. Its purpose was to establish and administer a system of industrial codes to control overpricing and regulate production, trade practices, and labor relations to offset the effects of the Great Depression and allow the nation to recover. The indifference, if not the outright racial hostility, of the NRA to the needs of the Black community earned it the Black epithet "Negro Run Around."

[Nov. 14, 1933]
Shubert Theater
Newark, N.J.

Dearest Langston—

I am as you see on the job. I heard from Gwyn said he was getting on all ok. And told me not to worry about him. We opened last night and had a wonderful crowd. And lots of applause. I am sending you the newspaper clipping. Every one is asking when you will be in N.Y.

I told Mr. Rockmore what you said and he said for you to come see the show if you don't come here he will bring the show out to you. Do you re-member Robt. Rockmore? He says he took you to dinner some time before you went away and he says he'd like to take you to his show.

Do you think you will be in New York this year?

I am in the dressing room with some "pains" some of them are ok some of them a "*pain.*" It is so funny how many people you can come in contact with—all different natures. Well I hope we will do some good so I can make a little money. It has been so tight with me the last two years. Homer will go over to Gwyn soon as he gets the money. I hope so for Gwyn needs some one with him. Yet I think he is doing fine and seems to be getting along nicely. Please write me a letter. I am always so glad to [be] here. Will have my mail sent from Toy's. Yours Mother.

——————————

[November 21, 1933]
Philly, Pa
Garrick Theatre
523 on S. 19th St.

Please send me a letter at *once*. Mamma

My Dearest—

I am sending you a Philly clipping. We opened last night with a won-derful house.[1] I hope that you will get to see the show while I am with it. I want you to send the money to Gwyn next time, and I think you need not send but $12.00 this time as I will take care of the rest if all goes well. After I get a start I can get along o.k. I think but this month I had lots to do as I was bare for clothes and must finish my debts. Just help me out a while. I don't like to ask you to do so much. I must try to send $10.00 to get Homer to Oberlin, so he can cook for Gwyn. Please write me at *once*. Mama

1. Carrie had a principal part as one of the Hunt sisters in Hall Johnson's play *Run, Little Chillun*. The original cast had 250 performers. Reviews were generally very good. One reviewer commented, "There are no stars. It is a finely concerted performance."

Oberlin, Ohio
Febr. 23, [1934]
Friday

My Own Boy.

You certainly made me inexpressibly happy when I received your telegram and your other token of love and good wishes. Oh it was so sweet of you and they were sure appreciated for I have been shut in so long that every thing brings happiness. About seven weeks I have been unable to go about, never before have I been so helpless. I am better, but the bone of the leg seems to get well very slow.[1] It is so weak, I can do very little on it. The Dr. said it would take time to heal, but it has been very slow, but I am so thankful it is not as painful as it was some nights. Now I rest all night with no pain but some days it still pains. But to get on this well, I guess I have been lucky. Because my age was against me. Any way, every one has been so kind to me, so good, the lady that lives under me was lovely. Nearly every day she fixed me meals when I was so bad, she would rub me and bathe me in hot water & turpentine and not being in this place long I never had many things but through kindness I have got on wonderful and I thank God for all.

I got a letter from Sallie this week. She is still planning on her brother James to come live with her. Ha! Ha! Says if he don't like Indianapolis she would pull up and move to Calif and you all could be together. *Lovely*. It took James a long time to need Sally and John. Hope they are very happy if they get located together.

I was reading a book "The Flutes of Shanghi"[2] and of the peach blossom time and the scarf was a lovely reminder of the same.

And that dear little ashtray that I sent Gwyn to get me a package of "Spuds" so I could celebrate with the tray. I love it and the Russian cigarette case.

And my friends every where have sent me letters and cards and I sure have not been forgotten and the cousins here are great. One of them a little flaxen haired girl of 11 years is my constant companion. She is here nearly all the time she's out of school. She has been so lovely to me. When I get well, and have money, I am going to take her to Cleveland (she's never been on the bus or train) and buy her an ice cream soda. She will be to happy to visit. She's very cute. Her name is Margie. Gwyn and her are great friends. We all play cards and pass some pleasant moments. It has kept me from many a lonely moment. Yet I've had lots of them. Gwyn seems doing well in school. He passed fine. Studies more. Write when you can.

Mamma.

Oh! Langston, I forgot to tell you, the lad in the house fixed sandwiches, potato salad, coffee and wine and invited some of the cousins in and made it very pleasant on my birthday for me. It was lovely of her. We had a nice time.

Pet has been quite sick. Amele had an operation and is spry as a bee racing around says nothing can *kill* her.

1. Carrie had seriously burned her leg in a cooking accident.

2. Louise Jordan Miln was the author of *The Flutes of Shanghai*, a novel published by Frederick A. Stokes Company of New York in 1928.

Oberlin, Ohio

Thursday

April 12 [1934]

[Upside page at top] That card from the Holy Land is lovely also necklace. Thanks. Please write me a *letter soon*.

Dearest Boy:

As I write you one of the best snows of the season is falling. Looks like February. Oh! It certainly makes one heart sick. Kit feels terribly over it for some reason. He has been promised a job in Cleveland and I do hope he gets it for he is so restless and I think work would help him. For he gets moods. He is some times the best and again the worst. I have said very little to you about Gwyn for in fact I do not see any thing one can do but some day when you are around him long enough you will know for yourself. I have done all I know for him, when I worked I gave him nearly every cent I made. Every one says he has too much honor but I don't know. When I see you I will talk it all over but if he gets work I hope it will all turn out for the best. I am better that is I can walk, but this weather has nearly got me. I have had a throat trouble for about three weeks. I do not know what it is but when I get so I can get to Cleveland I will go to the clinic.[1] There is no where [here to] find out. It is $2.00 round trip on bus to Cleveland and with my bills and rent, gas & eats, and Gwyn I can't get nothing yet to spare but hope to soon. Oh! If I was just at work some where. These times are terrible just making bums, desperadoes and gangsters out of the young people. Abbey Mitchell will be here Sunday for three days. I will be glad in a way to see her and entertain her as I have nothing to do so with, but will try to see her. If Gwyn works he will be gone three days out of a week Sat. Sun. Mon. I will be glad for most of the time I'm alone anyway sick and he will be making something. But Langston, neighbors, relatives and all have been so kind to me. I could not made it through this terrible winter if they had not stood by me. I will be so glad when I can see you. Thanks for all your loving kindness.

Mother.

Just got a letter from Homer.[2] The bus fare is about $11.00. 8 to Chicago and 3.50 to Cleveland. He can get no work there but I think he could if he could get here. Here is his letter. Do as you think best and can.

1. To have her burned leg treated.
2. He wrote her from El Paso, Texas, where he was working in a hospital. He claimed he was making only enough to pay his room and board.

———

Oberlin Ohio
July 10th

My Dear Langston:

I got your letter with both checks. Thank you very much. I will pay all debts. I will not cash the $30.00 until Aug 1st. Now Langston, I want you to come see me. Are you coming here & when?

How long will you stay!

If you are not I won't pay rent here as I cannot stay here alone this winter. I just cannot. I am not well enough. But will get a room some where, either Cleveland where Gwyn is, or Elyria. One cannot get a room in Oberlin and this is the only vacant house with cheap rent. I want to stay here until you come. Will you please let me know if you will come and stay a while, if so I'll clean this house up & be here when you come. Oh, Langston, I do want you to come. Please answer return mail these questions.

Mamma

So glad about your book. So glad for all your success.

Gwyn is doing nicely [double-underlined]. He is lovely with what he makes.

Ans at once or come

——————————

My Dear Langston:—

I am so pleased so shocked so everything that I don't know just what to say to you. Langston how could you spare me so much. Oh I certainly do thank you for it will make my trip glorious. I can't tell you in the words how I thank you. But I do feel very very thankful to you. I know now how much you love me. Darling I am so pleased—so happy. I will leave here on Wed Aug 8th. I will stop work here then so don't write any more here will be at Irene's a day or two for rest. Expect to leave Sat. write.

Your loving
Mother

——————————

Sat—

Dear Boy

Got your letter. Was all O.K. Gwyn has started foot ball and school also. He is all elated. He is one credit to the good. He has not got all his books. He lack French. We have the house looking pretty fair. He and I both worked very hard this morning to get straight and cleaned. There are a few things that we will have to get some time. But we are O.K. Now if we can just get work. We are both trying every day but every thing is so discouraging here.

I don't know what to do, they are only paying $3.00 per week in Cleveland for women's work. And so you see one can't make any thing any way. But it would beat nothing.

You can send check to same place as we have not moved our mail yet and we don't live far.

Much love. We will do the best we can. We have more cousins here—!!!

Mamma

––––––––––

[September 24]

Dear Lang

Your aunt's letter seems that she has been very ill. You better write her if you can.

Gwyn's birthday today. He is better. He made the foot ball and also Basket Ball [teams]. And got his hand cut today in a practice.

It is much cooler here today. Try and come home if you can before you leave. We and all here to see even if Zell[1] is there. What become of Jimmie?

Mrs. Colin Washington her mother got killed last Tuesday with a truck. Very sad. Write her.

Well you owe me a letter now.

Hope you write soon.

Yours Mother.

1. Zell Ingram, "a big, handsome, young black man . . . who lived with his mother over a popular Cleveland hot-dog shop," was Langston's friend and sometime driver and traveling companion (ARI 200–201).

––––––––––

Oct. 18, 1934
Oberlin, Ohio

My Dear Boy,

Just got your letter. Here is the way it is—George eats here. Georgia[1] rooms here. George buys the eats/ But I have to pay gas, Electric light and Rent. Now I was a little behind, but if you could send me a few dollars to catch up I would be o.k. I owe $3.50 Grocery bill—$2.85 gas. Then I pay $2.00 per month on Gwyn's suit. So you see, I was a little behind. I had the baby but I did not get paid for it. So it is gone and I'm glad. I will try to get along here. We have plenty to eat. I wish you could come home and stay a while, for we could live here for rent and gas also. Think it over. Gwyn is doing better this year in school. He'd better.

Love to you
Mamma

(over)

Green Pastures is in Cleveland on the 23rd and 24th of this month. I want to go. Could you send me enough to go on. If you have it. If not ok. But I do want to see it so bad. Write me at once.

Yours Mamma

P.S. Yes, we got the suit case and the Spread is *beautiful* [double-underlined]. I am crazy about it.

1. Here she refers to her cousins George Freeman and his daughter Georgia Freeman Payne. George was also raised in Lawrence, Kansas.

———— ————

Oberlin, Ohio
Thursday

We just got a big pumpkin for pies. Dad is still gone.

Mr. Dear Boy, I just came from the High School seeing "our Boy" Gwyn direct the High School Jug Band.[1] They gave a concert during the opening exercise period in the auditorium and I tell you "Kit" stepped on it he is a natural born orchestra leader. He was good. Everyone praised him and said that he was very graceful and full of rhythm. I say so. Neat and slicked up to beat the band.

Let me get you right on Geo or Georgia staying and eating here. George buys the food. *That's* [double-underlined] all I have to pay for Gas and rent. It merely transfers the food money to gas bill. So that's why I say you could come here & stay as food would not cost you anything at all and you could have a nice quiet winter. You could write plenty stories here for Rent and Gas and once more we'd be together. Better try it. We have plenty to eat.

Green Pastures will be in Cleveland and at the Ohio next Tuesday and Wednesday and the band will walk around. Georgia and I are trying to go and will if we get any money at all. Gwyn wants to go also but none of us have penny one. A man will take us on in his car for 40 cents a piece and then it is $1.00 to go in so there. Georgia is a real pretty soul. 22 years old. But has very little sense, but good hearted. Cousin Effie has moved. Erma has come from the South. Sherman Harvey died in Los Angeles last week. Auntie Reed is swell.

The baby is gone. The mother came and got it Monday. I am glad for it was lots of care and they would not pay. But it was a darling baby. He looked just like you when you were 7 months old. It is pretty cold or cool here now & George is bringing us a big coal stove and coal. Langston you should know George Freeman. Looks just like Uncle Henry only tall. Iron grey hair & cusses every one and is a funny character. You could write about him. He says for you to come here or write him a letter one for he don't care about little *niggers* like you. Write soon

Mamma

1. At Oberlin High School, Gwyn earned a letter—the "Oberlin O"—in sports but did not do well academically.

My Dearest: you all all O.K. I hope. Have you ate up your candy? I am leaving here Tuesday. On Friday night there will be a party of friends. I will leave Saturday. Helene wanted me to write you and tell you that Lincoln[1] is to have a benefit given for it at the Alhambra on Sunday night. Bo Jangles[2] is the headline. Called Lincoln University Benefit. I have a Stadium program but it is so large I can't sent it handy. I have just received as presents: from Mr. Jaffe sister a calf skin purse—from Mother Bath set—from Mrs. Jaffe Aunt—a strand of Jade (real) beads, from Another sister beautiful Black & orange Kimono, and a chiffon dress from Paris. Oh! I wish you could see it. It is gorgeous. Gwyn is here for the week as he needed shoes and I let him come to get them. I see me before I went west.[3] You don't mind do you? Could you write me here before Tuesday? Well much love to you. Write. Sorry I won't see you.

Yours lovingly
C M C

1. Lincoln University in Pennsylvania was Langston's collegiate alma mater.

2. Bill "Bojangles" Robinson (1878–1949) began dancing for a living at the age of six. He gained great success as a nightclub and musical comedy performer.

3. She means she wants Kit to see her before she goes west to visit relatives.

———————

Oberlin, Ohio
Nov. 1, 1934

My Dear Boy!

Just got your letter today and it seems you have gone again to the ends of the earth instead of coming home to see your poor old Ma.

Well again bad luck befell me. We have to move. *Have* to. The old poor white dame who owns this house got mad at the lady I rented from and put her out by law. (We have exactly 10 days to move). So of course I have to go also. I wrote you about it so I guess you know about it by now. I am moving in another apartment. Five rooms for $10 so I will take cousin

Georgia's daughter and she will pay $2.00 so I will only pay the same $8.00. It is a nicer place and I think will be warmer. There is a nice heater that goes with the place. So when the rent comes we'll be ready to move.

Gwyn's girl left today for Richmond so he is very heart sore tonight and I am not sorry but don't dare say so. Maybe he will study more. Thanks for the $5.00 first spending money I have had for 2 months. Sure was glad.

So you are in seclusion for 2 months. George said if you keep on fooling with him about coming home, he will back his truck up and load you on and bring you here. He sure is funny. Dad has been gone for weeks. God knows where. May be back out to Kansas.[1] Oh! Do you [know that] I hate to move but that's it. Will be better. All ok. The family I rent with is very nice. She was so good to me when I was sick. She's my pal. I am glad I can go to another place, where we'll be down stairs.

I have a note from a lady here will send to you. Their club wants you to speak for them.

Write at once
Your mother

We have to move Wednesday.

---

1. A November 15, 1934, letter from Homer indicates that he was still in El Paso.

Oberlin, Ohio
Sunday

Dearest Boy

Well the man is putting these people out where we live so we got to move—got to—I am so sorry. So I will try to get some place tomorrow. And as soon as you send money we'll be ready to move. Gee, I'm blue over it. Wish you'd come home am mad to see you now. Twice the teacher for Shaker Heights has driven down here. Says you were billed to speak there this next week also at the Civic Club. Is that so? And what happened? Why are you in Pens [Pennsylvania] every day? Girl or wife or what or divorce.

Please answer this at once.

Yours lovingly
Mamma

We had roast pork, carrots, potatoes, pie for dinner.

Oberlin, Ohio
Nov. 8th [1934]
Thurs.

Dear Langston,

I am sorry, so sorry to hear of James death. All of the misunderstandings are now wiped away and I sorrow much at his passing. Can't help it as he, after all, counting every thing was your father, the father of the only being in this world, that really belongs to me. Langston no one knows my life is and has always been so sad. I feel always now that there is nothing for me ever of happiness.

Langston I must be out of this house by next Tuesday.

Ten dollars will not get me moved or pay my rent anywhere else. So I don't know what to do or where to look. The cousins moved out yesterday, so Gwyn and I have no way to eat or get any gas or nothing. If I get another place here I have to pay $9.00 per month. I must pay for moving so now what can I do.

If you want us still to try to get a house and stay you will have to *wire* me at least $5.00 more.

We've never heard from Homer. Don't know where he is.

George built an extra room on his shack and took Georgia home, because his ex-wife was married again and the husband did not want Georgia, nor did any of them want to keep Georgia's little girl while she chased to school, and I could not keep her so Georgia went home with her father so she could take care of "Keets" the little girl—5 years old. So our food is gone. I have no one to cook for but Gwyn and therefore little to cook.

Let me hear at once as the court will evict the people and me also next week.

All of Life is such a muddle. I don't know what to do or say, and I am old and a pauper, and no use to anyone. I am just about given up the struggle. Answer at once so I will know what to do. Let me know if you must go to Mexico.

Yours,
Mother.

Nov 16, 1934
58 E. Vine St.

Dearest Langston,

I am moving today. We did not get the apt as I expected but we had to take a little old time house. But it will be warm and comfortable. I want to hear from you at once, if you fly to Mexico. Please be careful. The rent will be $9.00 but my gas will be less. Am so hurried. Will write again at once soon as I hear.

Mama

(over)

What were you messing around, according to papers, and get put out of San Francisco?[1] Tell me about it.

Answer soon ["soon" is double-underlined]

I spoke at church about you last eve.

---

1. Although Carrie did not reference specific news sources, she undoubtedly became aware of the radical political activities that culminated in threats on Langston's life. Early in 1934, Langston participated in a number of labor union and communist protests along the California coast, from Carmel to San Francisco; these events met with fierce opposition from strike breakers, vigilantes, and even police officers. His sympathy for the Communist Party was well known, especially to the newly organized Carmel American Legion Post. Langston's open advocacy, public performances, and supportive political tracts made him an easy target for those opposed to the rights of workers. At one contentious meeting between members of the John Reed Club and the Carmel American Legionnaires, he

discovered, to his dismay, that he was the only Black person present. Messages secretly delivered to him incited memories of two lynchings that had occurred in California that year. When word was quietly sent that a vigilante action was being planned against him, he did not hesitate to pack his belongings and slip out of town. We can only speculate about Carrie's knowledge of the details of the events that endangered her son's life. It is reasonable to conclude, though, that James Hughes's death, in one respect, was fortuitous, since it gave Langston a reason to leave for Mexico to help put James's business affairs in order.

Nov. 28, 1934
Oberlin, Ohio

My Dear Boy

Just got your card. Many, many thanks. I have had all your checks and Langston it seems I cannot hardly make it. We are now out of eats and fuel. The city won't help us. I went to see. They said if you were able to do anything and we non residents, they could not put us on their list and they considered it to bad to put your mother on city list. So that's talk and I am just about to leave here and hunt work some where. I don't know where. But I have done with out and been so bad off here, but maybe I can get something—I will try to finish.

Out this month until the next rent day, but Gwyn and I cannot go on this way. I am almost without clothes and we owe now for food and fuel, and Gwyn has got so worried he can't study so it's best to try to get out and help ourselves, if we can. I don't know whether with my bad leg I can do much but I must try. We thank you for all you have done, but we can't go on like this, some time no food scarcely. No money, and everything to worry you. I am nearly crazy. Gwyn is willing to work if he can get it and so am I. But Langston, this is too much on my nerves. I can't stand any more. Let me know when you go to Mex. Homer is in El Paseo [El Paso] working at a hospital. Write soon.

Yours,
Mother [double-underlined]

Kansas City, Kansas
[Dec 5, 1934]

My Dear Boys,

One and all. I am in Kansas City at last. Having stayed all night in Mo [Missouri] with Mollie I came over to Lot's [in Kansas] today. Will go back over to MO in a day or two, so when you write send letter to Mollie's place 1716 E 12th St. Palace Drug Store. She was so glad to see me. She looks fine. I came out here. It sure is quiet out here, seems like. Well. I wish I could hear Kit squall or Elmer eh! Eh! You say "Skip it". I do miss my sons so much tonight. I will go up to Lawrence maybe tomorrow. Kansas [City] both over here and in MO is very much changed, lots of new buildings and it just like another City. Built up wonderful. I had a lovely trip over from Chicago to K.C. It was my luck to meet up with the swellest Jewish lady and we ate together & we all went in the Ladies lounge to smoke and met others and one old man wanted me to set with him said his wife was an Indian & he knew I was. She liked me. We had lots of fun. The trip was short it seemed. Now I will write more later. Please let me know how you all are. Love & Kisses 1 2 or 3 a piece.

Please write

Ma

———————

Dec. 18th [1934]
Oberlin Ohio

My Dear Boy: You are so far away, and I feel so bad that you are way down there. And all for nearly nothing. Pray how old are those three ladies?[1] I truly am sorry you felt you had to go down there for I'd rather you came here. For at least we could have potatoes. I have nothing to buy you a present with. Coal and house rent and eats takes all I have, and then can't keep up. But I do the very best I can. Gwyn has been ill with a very severe cold.

He is some better today. He is studying hard this year and seems getting along. He is over anxious about Xmas. I am sorry. I don't know why. But he is still a great child in ways. I am not so good but knock around if I could only get work I know I'd feel much better.

I got the check. Thank you so much. I will try to give Gwyn what cheer I can. Merry Xmas to you but it breaks my heart with you so far away.

Yours lovingly,
Ma

1. Langston had gone to Mexico after his father's death. Here Carrie refers to the Patino sisters, one of whom collected rent money for James Hughes. Their relationship with him was fairly close, in part because of the rent-collecting job but also because they shared his sense of "aristocratic ideas regarding the peons," as Langston writes in *The Big Sea* (41–42). James left his estate to the sisters. His will contained no provisions for his estranged wife Frau Schultz, Langston, or other members of his family. Carrie was not surprised by James's snubbing, since he was displeased with everyone who disagreed with him.

———————————

I have a dream keeper.[1] The anthology & everything else you sent. It has been so cold here this month. We nearly froze up too. We burn coal and Gwyn nor I know much about it and how to keep fire but we just trying to learn.

Langston, you have lots of engagements, to speak up here. The Oberlin College, Some womens Club, Shaker Heights School, Community Center & several want you. I wish you'd come from there home. Please try anyway.

Write soon.

Yours Ma

1. Langston's poetry collection *The Dream Keeper*.

———————————

[December 25, 1934]

Dearest Boy:

This is the third Xmas morn that finds me alone, no one to even say Merry Xmas to. I am just awful lonely. Gwyn left Saturday for Richmond Va. I was all alone since. I worked Xmas Eve and am at work now but every one has left here, so I am still alone.

I am ashamed to tell you that Gwyn must take $27.00 of the money and went to Richmond. He has been half sick for a month and so down. I don't know what he'd have done if he had not gone. I did all I could to keep him from going but all in vain. So I paid my Gas bill, payed some on Gwyn's suit. So I had no Xmas. But it's all O.K. I am not a bit worried only that I could not make Gwyn see the foolishness of his act. Oh! He is in love & crazy about that girl and there is no sense in him. Bessie & Amele invited me over to Cleveland for dinner but I could not go. There is a terrible big snow here today real Xmas weather. Langston the only thing in this world I hope for is to live to see you once more. Oh! I do want to see you. I am just fixing to leave the place I worked to go home and make fire & sit down for a rest. Then I will go to get some bacon & eggs. I am so all in I am hardly hungry. Georgie got your card & was very happy over it. I guess you will hear from Gwyn. He said he would write you. Told him he must. Did you get the picture?

Yours

Mother

Very Merry New Year.

Langston I felt your father would do just as he did. But its all right. You played away and he was not pleased.

Things Fall Apart
1935

The year 1935 proves to be, arguably, the lowest point in Carrie's life. If the thirty-three letters she writes to Langston are any indication—the most in any of the twelve years represented here—her precipitous fall following her stint on stage signifies she has reached rock bottom. The pressure she puts on Langston to fuse more fully with her and Gwyn increases exponentially. Strategically, she focuses on four themes in an effort to force him to accede to her needs and demands: (1) Gwyn's life, (2) her increased loneliness, (3) the discovery of a tumor in her breast, and (4) poverty so grave that she might have to resort to living on a county poor farm.

The death of Langston's father, James Hughes, on October 22, 1934, incurs an additional obligation for Langston. He returns to Mexico in December to assist James's longtime friends and heirs to his estate, the Patino sisters, in settling James's will and business affairs. Not to be outdone in her perceived contest for Langston's affections, Carrie forces his trip to become an emotional tug of war. Beginning in January 1935, she writes passionately, pleading for Langston to return to Oberlin because she desperately needs him. The initial strategy is to elicit Langston's sympathies by using Gwyn's poor health and even poorer academic performance as emotional appeals. "I am very much worried about Gwyn," she writes. "He is so thin and pale and has so little to build on." Since Langston is "so far away," she feels compelled to worry "just nearly to death with every thing." Gwyn, she frantically implies, vacillates between noble pursuits and moral dissolution: wishing to write, acquiring money, desiring marriage, and consuming too much liquor. That he relapses into poor health three more times increases her anxiety and helplessness. Utterly frustrated with Gwyn, she throws up her hands and cries: "I am alone with him night and day and sometimes I feel I can't go on then I spruce up and try it again." In a telling coda, she softens a bit: "I guess many mothers has done the same." How ironic she should invoke maternal instinct as an argument for supporting Gwyn when the pattern of "abandoning and returning" defines the relationship she had with Langston when he was Gwyn's age.

The maternal instinct toward Gwyn that she carefully displays evolves into another connectional strategy with Langston. "If he goes," writes Carrie about Gwyn's desire to seek employment in another city, "it will leave me alone for the first time in my life." Once again her feelings occupy center stage. With a tone of self-pity, she beseeches Langston: "[I] hate to live alone so if Gwyn goes I will have to hear what you think best for your lonely little Mother." No doubt the pathos dripping from these lines appears to be sincere, but the effect is emotional manipulation. Her words also render invisible and, hence unimportant, Langston's emotional needs. At no point does she acknowledge the many times Langston lived alone when she was off following her dreams or her man.

Gwyn's poor health and her increased loneliness when he leaves exacerbate another problem for Carrie: her deepening impoverishment. Rhetorically, she frames her condition masterfully into an emotional dilemma. Faced with eviction and no place to go, she desperately writes: "I am again at the place I can't go and I can't stay." This one phrase succinctly captures Carrie's life at arguably her lowest point. In trying to hold on to Gwyn and provide also for herself, she tells Langston: "Now the problem is what and where and when, If I am to have Gwyn. I don't know where to stay." The power of these appeals, in Bowen terms, is actually a test of the degree to which the family has successfully bonded. The fundamental question is how will the family bond to solve a problem that has been properly identified as threatening their unity and still emerge from the crisis with self-differentiation. Carrie elects a strategy that proves to be inappropriate enmeshment. She divests herself from any blame for their problems or any responsibility for finding a workable solution when she shifts the burden for a remedy onto Langston's shoulders. On one hand, she assumes a business stance and sends him a proposal to buy a house, one that would be large enough to accommodate all three of them comfortably, but seeing this tactic as ineffective, she reverts to emotional manipulation. She holds Langston emotionally hostage by declaring that since she cannot go or stay, her only solution is to go "on out to the Poor farm & end it all." She increases that dire threat, which plays on his emotions, by blackmailing him—hinting at possible actions that would harm the family's reputation and, more crucially, Langston's image: "I hate to do that for I am [your] mother & everyone knows it and I don't want to hurt you." Her manipulative words set the terms of the decision Langston must make.

As heartrending as the prospects of ending it all in "the poor house" are, Carrie's discovery of a "blood tumor" in her breast signals the possibility that she will be freed from such earthly concerns as rent, food, gas, coal, and water. Putting more pressure on Langston, she writes: "I do want to see you and I wanted you to come while I felt fairly well. For this tumor gets no better and I am getting worried about it. If you can I wish you could come home." With Langston still in Mexico, Carrie recognizes that she's in a fight for her life. The doctor treats her with a procedure that Carrie calls "hypodermics" in an effort to reduce the size of the tumor. She frantically seeks Langston's presence so that together they can decide whether an operation or some other form of treatment might be more effective, but the medical problem gets folded into the problem of living accommodations: "I want to keep the house if I can[,] at least until you come home. Then I may get a room if you won't stay with me awhile." She makes the arrangement more inviting by saying he could work on his novel "in this beautiful little town" (Oberlin) and that they "could have a month or so of happiness together. . . . I'd love to have you just a little while once in my life."

[January 8, 1935]
Friday

Dear Langston

I am very sick. I can't stay here on these people. They have no money and only the wife working. Irene very ill. Me very ill. No one to wait on me. No one to do one thing. I am practically helpless. I must try to get home. I am too sick to travel on bus. Don't know how I will get along. Much love. I'd love to see you. But don't know how this will turn out.

Dr. has done no good. I can't stand much more pain.

When I can will write you. I can't do any more now. I can get no food hardly. No one to fix nothing and I am suffering so. Course they do what they can but have nothing to do with nor me either. Hall went to see how I was. I told him.

Yours
C——

[envelope]   Jan. 20, 1935
107 W 114 St. Apt. 10
New York, NY
Jan 3.
Air Mail

Mr. Langston Hughes

———————

Jan 9th, 1935
Oberlin

Dearest Boy,

Just a line to tell you that Gwyn has been very ill since the First. He had a very severe case of flu and as yet is too sick to enter the new term of school. He is terribly discouraged. He has taken lots of medicine, but the Dr. says it was a bad case, so he is still quite sick. I felt I should have written you before but I expected every day he would improve.

I have not heard from you for two weeks what is the matter. Did you enjoy the Xmas? I did not have nothing much was alone all the while. I hope you are ok. I am very much worried about Gwyn. Hope he gets better soon. He is so thin and pale and has so little to build on. Well, I must mail this as I have not had any eats yet. It is about 9:30 though but I have not been up long, so I am awake during the night and I am not so well myself.

Yours lovingly,
Mom

Oberlin, Ohio
January 14, 1935

Mr. Dear Langston,

I just got your letter after worrying my self to death about you. For fear you were either sick or something I sure am sorry to hear you will stay on there until March. I don't see why, but maybe you know best. But, Oh Langston, it seems you are so far away and I am here worried just nearly to death with every thing.

I did not get the money order for the $20.00, that is the second one misplaced here for me. One sent me when I had the baby. There is a set of thieves in this post office. They take out money orders all the time but can't be caught. Yes, I got the $40.00. I got the $16.20. Gwyn got the $5.00 making a total of $61.20 instead of $81.20 that would have squared us up great.

Of course as I told you before Gwyn must go to Richmond. He is crazy about that girl and he came back very very sick and he has sure been very sick. He missed last week school so sick he could not go. Langston, I think the strain is too much for you and it is becoming too much more for me. Sometimes I have nothing to buy coal, no money for eats. Now I have just 34 cents and gas and lights due again. Oh! it is all harassing the life out of me. I can't stand it. I think if I do I will break and go heck. Gwyn is terrible unhappy and restless. He wants to write, he wants money, he wants liquor, & he wants to get married and I am just nearly out of my mind sometimes.

If I can go any where and get work if I only get 50¢ a week, I can't live like this. I don't know how to show you how things are because I hate to worry you, but I can't go on like this unless I am just sent to the asylum.

I could not buy a Crisis if I want to every so much and I never want to read anything ever about Oberlin. If I ever get away from it I'll wash my hands of it forever. It's the narrowest "counfoundedst" talking, lying, mean, contemptible hole in God's whole country. Oberlin Eh! I hate the whole name. I've had more trouble, more worry, more everything here. No more for me.

Sad about Wallace Thurman and Rudolph Fisher's death. Poor boys.

While I am here writing the water man comes to collect $1.79 and that he will have it shut off. I told him o.k. as I had no money. That's the way it is all the time. Next the Gas & Light will be off. Well I am just sick of it all. Why try to do and everything in the world is against you.

Please track the $20.00 and let me know at once.

Mother.

———————

Oberlin, Ohio
January 15th

Write at once [double-underlined]

My Dear Langston,

Again "I take pen in hand" to write you and I hope it will be more coherent as I was so worried when I wrote yesterday I did not know what I really said. Well, "worry will kill you," but I am still here and alive but I have been through some.

Well, I am now to my humiliation and embarrassment on government relief. Oh, Langston it broke my heart but I had to eat and I had to have coal. As Gwyn was to fault of this, he is in the depths of "misery and de-spair." If he had not "just Gone" to Richmond we would be all ok but go he must. So see. Well, Life is a funny pain after all. Now I can get "eats & coal." No rent or gas or lights. The poor is supposed to live with out either.

Ha! Ha! I had a fight to get any help. The Negroes exploded on the fact I had a "wealthy" son that you were in Hollywood almost playing with Joan Crawford & Clark Gable. Ha! Ha! So, of course, they wanted proof I wasn't get $1,000 a month sent. Well, enough said, I get salt pork & bacon, (which I can't eat as I have no teeth). Well, if you pay rent and gas, perhaps I can hold on if I can keep Gwyn in the fold, it seems almost a useless, thankless job, but he has been meeker since his illness.

Langston, this is a bum pen. Belongs to some of Gwyn's gals. But I wanted you to know. My own Darling that I know you are doing all you can, but it is an untold worry to me to see you work, work & sacrifice. I am old. I can get the old age pension soon, a few years, but I am willing to try to make it or go to the poor house one and die amid poor humiliated poor like my self, but to save you my dear boy, You are a wonder, an angel, and I *love* you more than I do my life and I must help you instead of hinder you and I must get out and stop being a constant draw. Gwyn must get out and make a man of himself. He never will be any good maybe not then. He is *wild*. He wants "wine, women & song" maybe he will change.

Now Langston. Forgive & forget the "wrango" [rant] I wrote in the other letter. I never got the $20.00 so you had better look that up. Where did you send it from. Let me know at once. And I can see if it ever came through here & *what date*!! Please hunt it for it will fix me just right for now.

Please forgive you old mother and love her for she *loves* you and *loves* [double-underlined] & *loves* [triple-underlined] you. Oh! Langston in my heart you are all. You and my life. God and you. That's *all*. I am glad you liked the picture. When I get money I will send the Patinos one. Give them my love. Tell them I am "wading through the deeps" but hope to come out "more than conqueror." One of the cousins old man Pettiford died, but I can't go; have no way to go yet as I know of. He lived 14 miles in the country up to Wakenisan. Well. So long

Darling I pray God keeps you always.

———————

Oberlin, Ohio
January 25th [1935]

My Dear Boy,

Jus received the order from Laredo, Texas. Thanks I am on the trace of the other one. It came to Oberlin all ok. And was cashed.

Well Gwyn has been very ill this week and still is. He seems to go back instead of get well. Now a new feature has developed on top of the cold. He cannot hardly walk or stand straight and seems to have inflammation of the Bladder. Poor child. He sure has had a long, painful siege of it. He will see the Dr. again today—of course the City Dr. He's took an awful lot of medicine.

I am just knocking along sorry you have to be worried with me and all the ills of the family at this end. I wish I could help it all. For I am sorry for you, better you were married with 10 kids. They wouldn't worry you no more. I can't go to Cleveland just now but will later. I can't leave Gwyn alone. I am holding on trying with all my might to keep him from flying off on a tangent. So far I can kinder hold him but if I leave him—Well. Good Bye to all hopes. Will write more later. Am in a hurry.

Mamma

If you come to Oberlin we could live cheap.

———————

Oberlin Ohio
Feby 3rd
Sunday evening

Dearest Boy, I am very lonely tonight. I have been house in all day, as I was ill last night and felt "punk" all day. And it snowed and got very cold, so here I am. It will probably be below zero before morning.

We have had a very hard winter so cold. And slick sidewalks. Miserable, miserable, so bad you could not go out, even if I had any place to go, which isn't often.

Well, I hate to write this letter, worse than I ever hated to write to you, for I am sure it will be a letter that will be very disappointing to you but

Oh! You should realize how terrible I feel over the whole affair. I told you Gwyn has been very sick out of school three weeks. He got better took some of the tests, and of course, did not pass. Well, in October Gwyn was suspended, for having the tiff with the foot ball coach, cursed him and cut classes for fun. Well, I got him back in school, on condition that he stop cutting classes, that he pass in four studies, and could not play foot ball. But he continued to cut clases, had 24 days absence, and did not pass, so of course the Principal suggest that he does not return to school. I am sorry to write this but cannot help to do so. I see nothing now to do but let Gwyn go to work. If he can get it to do. He is not the boy he should be, but I'd hate to see him outdoors. So, if you can let us stay here until I can get work or something. It is so cold I think I will have to stay here until March. If you can do this, just rent & gas. I want work so bad. But I will have to see what I can do. Gwyn will have to work also.

Mamma.

Gwyn has had the bad luck to fall in the worst class of boys here, he has run around and drank whiskey and generally got his system poisoned and it will be some time before he is well. It is too bad, but I have talked and prayed pleaded but all to no avail, but now he sees his mistake, sees his wasted days sees what he could do. Oh! I am sure sorry, so sorry for the boy. He couldn't see. But what's he's to do. You have done your share. Your part and it's all a shame things did not turn out different. But Gwyn's antecedents are against him I am afraid. Poor boy, so foolish! But when he gets on his own he will find life different. He head was so hard he could hear nothing. I have done all I could, sacrificed worked talked. You have done all you could. So I have been to the end of my rope.

Please write me at *once*. I am worried & sorry over it all.

February 6, 1935
Oberlin, Ohio
Wednesday

Dear Langston,

Just to tell you Gwyn has a third relapse and is flat of his back again, with fever and chill. Today I could get no medical aid. As the city told the Drs. to go out no more until again notified as to where they will be paid. So that's that & also this. I am so worried, blue & sad, so sorry for poor little sick Kit. I can hardly stay up my self with back ache. But have to try.

Yours,
Mamma.

Answer at once.

––––––––––––

I know Langston you will be so glad never to hear of us who are such a worry to you. I feel sorry for you to.

Oberlin Ohio
Feby 16th Saturday

My Dear Boy:—

I am so glad to hear from you. I had had a heart rendering week. Gwyn, poor little fellow has suffered death and his fever about 104 or 105 and just me sitting here alone, doing all I could, maybe he could not get any sleep or rest until 5 or 6 in the A.M. I am worn out. But he is better yesterday and today. I am so glad, for he could not lived long as he was. Dr. says now he must be still and nothing straining for a month. He will sit up tomorrow. Has only had liquids for a week. Langston, me and my bad leg has sure stood a terrible two weeks. Gwyn was sick since New Years Day. Had his first chill then.

I got the Max Lieber check—for $29.70. Thank you. I was so glad of a little month. For my Gas was about to be cut off. Now I will pay rent & light and as I get food don't have to buy that. The neighbors have been fine to us. But George Freeman, my own cousin, never gave us an apple. What is the matter I don't know. He seems awful funny lately. Sorry but I don't know whats the matter. Aunt Lucy & Cousin John were lovely also the other relatives.

I did not get the $20.00 yet. It was traced here to this office but can't seem to find out who cashed it. They are working on it they say. But all those officials are sure *dumb*.

When Gwyn is able to be around I will try to decide what to do. I am not as strong as I was but can work some where. Of course, Gwyn will have to try to get work somehow. He was going to go to relief camp but can't now, for he can't pass the examination. Gee, wish I could see you & talk everything over. Wish I could be with you for awhile.

Yours
Mother.

[Carrie sends Langston an advertisement for razor blades]

> NOT MADE BY GILLETTE
> Sold in Better Drug Stores
> (Attention!! Your druggist is authorized to guarantee you satisfaction with D Blades. Use one blade from a package. If it isn't the keenest you ever used, return the other four blades and your money will be refunded.)
> THE D BLADE CO.
> Cleveland, Ohio

[On back of advertisement]

> ALL MY LIFE
> I have been bawled out, balled up, held up, held down, bull-dozed, black-jacked, walked on, cheated, squeezed and mooched; stuck up for war tax, dog tax, cigarette and gas tax, Liberty Bonds, baby bond and matrimony, Red Cross, green cross and double cross, asked to join the G. A. R., Women's Relief Corps, Men's relief and stomach relief; I have worked like Hell, soles on my shoes nearly gone, I have been drunk, gotten others drunk, lost all I had and part of my furniture and because I won't spend or lend all of the little I earn and go beg, borrow or steal, I have been cussed and discussed, hung

up, robbed and damn near ruined and in spite of it all, instead of being cut and scraped, butchered and carved by cheap razor blades, the only reason I am happy today is because I use Double-edge—

———————

Oberlin Ohio
Feby 23—

Dearest Boy:—

Yesterday one year ago I was housed unable to walk. This year Gwyn, poor little soul, is so poorly so thin, so weak, every day it seems he's going farther away from me, the only mother he ever knew. I have done all I could. I am nearly work out. But if he'd only get well. My birthday was full of trouble and pain two years. I hope soon to hear of you being nearer.

Oh! For two days, in fact a week the weather is terrible, blizzard & snow and Gwyn has been so cold. I've kept all the fire I could but he is so thin. If he gets better I will try to make some plans as it is now he is the only problem.

Write. Yours
Mother.

He sat up a little bit and got chilly, he took another cold. I had the Dr. again Tuesday night, he said he thought Gwyn had a little more resistence this time. What he would probably pull out this spell (the 4th) better. I do hope so. Oh, Langston. I am alone with him night and day and sometimes I feel I can't go on then I spruce up and try it again.

I guess many mothers has done the same.

———————

Dear Langston

I did not want to say this to you but I have to. I must tell you how terribly Bessie has treated me since I have been sick and she treated me bad enough before.

Not once has she been up here to see me unless I called her. For I would stand crooked. I can't get me anything to eat until way in the P.M. for I am so ill. She has never been the one to fix me a little something out to me. Today it is 4 and I wanted something so bad asked the little girl to go and she would not let her. She had to scrub, wash dishes & all things, great God how can any one treat one that way and I've been so ill. She has the meanest streak or just plain dumb. Every one that comes here says this. I know Mrs. Brown takes good care of you all these nights. I have been so sick and not once has she even come to ask me how I was or tend one moment. She knows most of the time I have not been able to walk the steps. She will lay the mail down the stairs & its generally afternoon when I get it. Oh! She is I can't tell you how anyone can be that way. I've always paid her, tried to be nice to her but not one favor will she do me.

Please write or let me know when you can come. I won't pay her this rent for she is so nasty.

Kit can't bear her.

[March 8, 1935]
Oberlin, Ohio
58 E. Vine St.

My dear dearest Boy,

I want so much to write to you, but it seems I don't know much to say. Gwyn is better. He is going about some, but I do not want him to be too fast and get back again. There is several cases of severe sickness in our immediate neighborhood. One of our many cousins is very sick, just below our house. He had pneumonia.

The weather here is very cold and sleety today. This has been a very long winter it seems. I had a letter writing fit tonight and did not want to leave you out.

Gwyn is in a frenzy to go to the city of Cleveland to hunt work. If he goes it will leave me alone for the first time in my life. But I do not know yet what to go at or what to do. There is no work here. I could not just sit here alone. I am able to work some, so think may be I'd better to go where I could work. My letters I don't want to make you sad, but Darling, I have had some sad times here when Gwyn was so sick, but I am sure glad he's better. But Langston, don't worry about me. The Lord will prepare some way. I don't want you to worry at all. When Gwyn gets work, then I will do something. I don't know yet.

Will write more later.

I will write you again soon. I do not know yet just what best to do and I must stay some where, but hate to live alone so if Gwyn goes I will have to hear what you think best for your lonely little Mother. Mother had best do. Oh Langston I love you so and I do want to see you. I wish I could live with you or where you are and I'd never worry again.

Mom
Write soon

Tell Patinos I will write them now soon I've had no time.

———————

Oberlin Ohio
March 10 [1935]

My Dear Langston

Have intended to write but have wanted to wait to see what Elmer done.[1] He has not been going to work on time. Mr. Jelliff had to come for him and wake him up last night and was he mad. He said I don't know what to do with him. He was disgusted. He went off to get his pay at noon, and it was past 8 P.M. and no Elmer. Of course I don't expect one cent and out he goes.

I am sending you your mail tomorrow. Got a letter from Kit. He was very much impressed with you in Dayton and says "you were wonderful." Pray what did you do! Effie is still here. But must get a room. I can't stand her & Tom and all that. Big snow here today. It was all a mistake about the fire escape. No such thing. Man just got tired and I think owed rent. Told when to move. Raynor is working. He has been over every night. Tired out. Wish he'd come now and go hunt Elmer.

All O.K. out he goes. People shan't impose on you. Not & me stand by. *Well just* got the money from Elmer. $23.00. One of the boys brought it out. Write to me soon.

Mama.

Money from Checking account $183.00

Jany 3rd 1935

Kit	$26.00
Back Rent	20.00
Rent Present Month	20.00
Hospital	8.00
Dr. Freedman (med)	3.00
Grocery Bill	12.00 (4 weeks)
Grocery Bill	2.60 (2 weeks)
Paid "on Kit's" overcoat	5.00
Langston (sent to)	20.00
Telephone to Langston	3.00
	$118.60

I'll write you before though

I will pay now 2 months rent. Move and that won't cost very little. Oh! Even this is so much better. $3 cheaper. Near town, I can't carry water much more. I've tried to find something and this is a find. Between Ivade Park & Euclid and Cory.

Write me here until Feby 1st.[2] Then write to 7918 Cory

---

1. The relationship between Elmer and Carrie is not clear. Quite possibly a paramour, he lives with Carrie on and off until 1937. On May 5, 1937, Kit writes to Langston that Elmer is "nasty" to Carrie and "jealous," saying that even though Carrie had asked him to leave several times, he had refused until Carrie threatened to call the police. In this letter, Carrie refers to the work Elmer does for Russell and Rowena Jelliffe, who own the Black theater, Karamu House. He builds stage sets for them. Carrie spells their last name variously, most often without the final "e."

2. She must have meant April 1 because her letter is dated March 10.

~~Feb~~ March 12th
Oberlin Ohio

Dear Boy:—

Your letter came also the $20.00. I have never got the other order yet. I will tell you about it when I see you. When? I was called up to the relief Station today again to find out how I was now situation so they will still give me food (some) and coal, of course they don't give enough food for Gwyn & I for two weeks, but when I have money I have to buy more. But we will get along now. For when I can pay my rent and gas all o.k. I am paying a dollar or so on my debts also. But of course I need clothes terribly but if I get some where and get a little work I can possible get some clothes.

Oberlin has been in the limelite this week. Two prominent persons died. My friend's mother. Then the only colored mail carrier, went to shoot his wife and they had lots of notoriety. All disturbed. I have a cold, but am doctoring it. Gwyn's is better, but is listed for X-ray tomorrow. Well Guess I have told everything. The "Lord" of Green Pastures is ill. Green Pastures closes next week indefinitely. So Arthur from N.Y. wants me. He says I should come to N.Y. and get an apartment. But it takes money to start in a big house. Gwyn wants to get work soon as he can. Says he will go away some where. I don't know where.

Now darling I am going to bed. Write soon, tell me you will be home.

Yours lovingly,
Mamma.

——————

Oberlin, Ohio
March 29 [1935]

My Dear Boy,

I have waited each day to hear from you, but it seems so long and I have not heard one word. I guess you are still down there.

Well, for the first time I am all alone. Soon as Gwyn got better, he went over to Cleveland and now after two weeks, he writes me that he has a job and is going to stay. So that leaves me all alone with the house and I am not fond of being alone at all. If I could only get a little work here I would try to stay but I can't get anything at all to do, so I am just at a stand still as to know what to do. If you were only coming this way or if I could only come to you for a while when you get some where. Please write me at once for I want to know what you say. Gwyn and Milton Parks are in a little place in Collinwood, and they want to live alone. So I can't even keep house for them. I have two alternatives. One go to Cleveland and rent a room, try to get work, another go to N.Y. and knock around there and work, but I am getting old. I can't pull around so much as I used to. But either of these are the only things open to me just now.

I must work and get money to go in an Old Folks home. Some time when I get disabled and older. Poor Homer, I have not heard of him all winter. A man in Cleveland told me Homer had a very bad spell while over there. But no one knows where he went or where he is. Perhaps dead. Oh! Langston such a poor pen. I need a fountain pen very badly. I had beans, potatoes, fish, for supper. Wish you were here. Everyone asks for and of you. I need glasses so much. My eyes hurt me very much. Guess welfare board will get them for me. May be.

Well, I am so sleepy. Guess I'll play a game of solitaire and retire. Poor old Man Harrison so long the "Lord" had to leave us. Largest funeral in N.Y. and Chicago ever.

Please write me soon. Hall's choir of "Run Little Chillun" passed through here Tuesday. They sang at Fort Wayne, Ind.

Much, much love

Your Mother—

C——

Oberlin, Ohio
April 15 [1935]

My Dear Boy,

Just received the letter and the $13.50 very glad to get it as Gwyn was fretting me sick to get to go deposit on his uniform. He has been to Cleveland since last Friday. Now Langston, I do hope you don't feel I am just worrying you to death for I don't want to. I wish I could write you lovely, sunny letters but Langston, my life is so drab. I can't get up any good feeling any more. I am not well. The weather was very cold today with much snow, so I can hardly get around on my leg at all and it is so painful.

I have decided it is best to stay here now, until you get here any way. I can get food. I can't get any house rent or gas or light money, but $12.00 per month will cover that so if I can get my rent up, I will stay right here. For I don't know how I could get through much work just now. After I see you, then we can decide. I am willing to go out to the county farm here and I won't cost anyone a cent. If not, I will stay here, try to have rent and gas, and get along. Oberlin is a nice home town and if I could pay my debts here I'd love to just keep this little house and stay. Maybe later I could get a welfare child and I would not be alone all the time. They pay $4.00 per week. And if I could get caught up, I could live on $12.00 per month. With relief food. Now if when you get it, you could send me two months rent and $5.00 for Gwyn's suit and $4.00 for medicine I owe. I'd be rather straight and if you could send me $10.00 per month and Gwyn works, I could get along now. If that suits you, I will just stay here for I must have some where or go to the county farm. I hate to do that for I am you mother & everyone knows it and I don't want to hurt you. I can't go anywhere I have no clothes. I have no dress no stockings, nothing to go anywhere. I could not go to N.Y. this way. I have to wait until I get some thing.

Now you write let me know, if that arrangements strikes you as ok. I am so sorry so sorry I have to tell you or worry you with it all. I saw you award in the N.Y. Times April 8th 1st page. Stating it was $2,000.00 also Grant Still. Good for you both.[1]

Please come on here. It is so nice and quiet. You'd enjoy it here. It is beautiful in the summer. Let me know if you won't come on here. Don't stay in California. Please come see me. I need to see you so bad. My darling baby. All I have in this world. Please come home. I want to see you so much. So much.

Yours,
Mamma.

Please write soon and tell me you will be *Home* [double-underlined] to see *Mother* [double-underlined] Please.

1. Both Langston and William Grant Still were awarded the prestigious Guggenheim fellowship in 1935. For Still, the fellowship was an extension of the one he was awarded the previous year for musical composition. Langston proposed to work on another novel, thus Carrie's several entreaties for him to return to Ohio where he could share a house with her and create virtually undisturbed.

———————

Oberlin, Ohio
April 27th [1935]

My Dear Langston.—

I am so glad to hear from you today, that I will write you a letter at once. We are all well and I am so lonesome to see you that I feel that you have been gone for a month already.

As you predicted Elmer did not get but a little money, and as yet has no job and he is still running around telling every one that he has a great job, with the art department and that he will go to work there and you you should hear how Mr. Jelliff is still saying the same he told you that he cannot work at any thing that does not come through him, so I do not know at all what it will all turn out to be. Ha. Ha.

I want you to go to see Arthur while you are there, so I am sending you the address, he will be so glad to see you and you tell him that I will be looking for him to stop when they come back, and tell Hall the same.

I saw Raynor, Mason, and all of Kits friends, on Sunday but I tell you that our boy has changed and I hope for the better. The other pair of pants

you gave me is Elmers, and not Kit's. The weather here has been terrible
since you have been gone. I have some letters that came for you but they
are no good I don't think so I do not send them.

I sent your Laundry that same day. Did you get it? Old Blunt is still
here after the fire, the stove up stairs exploded the other day and burnt the
woman up stairs. Gloria sent you a winter scarf. It is very beautiful. I had
bread pudding today and I felt very sorry you was not here as you like it
so much. We also had an old lamb breast that I like very much if it is dry
and hard. Elmer is now working the Puzzles. I will be glad that he will be
getting at least $1,000.00 for them

Mother.

Mr. Jelliffe said he just sent your checks to. So glad you saw Carrie &
Maude. I would love to see them and Mel's babies. I know they are sweet.
I was over to Baymond Mothers last eve & that "kid" I'd hug her long ago.
Had!! Write to me soon again.

Oberlin, Ohio
May 2nd [1935]

My Dear Son—

With your letter came a demand to vacate the house—of course I have
a few days to do so. I guess so. I will owe two months rent the 13th. But
the old lady is a crank. But she is not the only one losing rent. But all o.k.
I will get another place and be all right for I want to stay here I have good
friends here. But poor—But kind. And I am not so well. I need quiet and
try to be with out worry. Well, I am so glad for you and I hope you will
enjoy every dollar of the amount for you have worked very hard, long and
faithfully. So may you have great joy. And if I could only see you is all I
ask in life then I do not care much. I am so lonely here in the house alone.
Gwyn is working. He is in a hat store in Cleveland. I gave him enough to
pay room rent & get eats & he did not seem to care much about the run,
but he says he may take it. But he does fare I guess, nothing much. OH!
Darling don't change your mind to come see me. Soon as you can. I will be

so glad to have you. Let me know when you leave. The 2nd Sunday in May is "Mother's Day." I have received your love always the time and continually pray for you and thank God for my dear son, such a darling son as you are. I know you love me and do all you can for me. You will never never suffer for you have been so good to your poor old mother. Love to Charles & Patina's. Wish I could see them.

Well, Darling you had better write Shaker Height school and make a date that would be good money & they do want you so bad. Teachers have worried about when you'd be here. College here also wants you. If you want to you could clear up quite a little here & in Cleveland. Of course, that is if you want.

Write very soon. For I will count the days until you come up to this dear old town to see me. Darling, I'd be so Happy.

Your lonely Mother
C. M. H. C.

———————

[May 14, 1935]
Oberlin, Ohio
Monday May

My Dear Boy:

Just got your letter with $30.00. And as so glad but in hopes you would have left Mexico.

Well last Tuesday I went to the Dr. I have a very bad blood tumor on my breast, for which they arc giving me hypodermics to reduce it. I just got on the couch and your letter came. Now you must come home some time, soon as you can for if this method is not successful I will have to go to the hospital for either operation or something. I want you home. I hope it gets o.k. but I had a slight hemmorage from it and had to have the Dr. I want to keep the house if I can at least until you come home. Then I may get a room if you won't stay with me awhile, for I must have some one in the house with me now. Why couldn't you write your novel here in this beautiful little town and we could have a month or so of happiness together for Langston I'd love to have you just a little while once in my life. Gwyn is there in Cleveland with a little job not doing much. He is making very little. But he seems to get along. He is much worried just now about me & my illness. Mother's day came and I got no card. No remembrance of any kind and I was so blue. All alone. Every one else got flowers, card something. No one remembered me.

Please come home. Answer at once what you will do. Every letter you put it off farther and farther. Please don't stay down there so long. I was praying you'd be back at least in Cal. Answer this letter at once. I'll pay back rent & gas. All else can go. Answer at once.

Yours lovingly
Mamma

Oberlin Ohio
Thursday

Dear Langston:—

Just got your letter. I am very glad for you that you got a Guggenheim Fellowship. It will be of great help to you. And I am glad for you.

As you will see by Gwyn's letter he has a job but held up for 5.00 for uniform. He wants to work so bad. So hope you can help him start. If I can ever get straight and get out of debt Here I would not mind staying. But some how I have to get straight or next month I will have to go to the poor farm. And it will be all right I won't care at all. At least all my worries will be over and I will be at peace at least won't have to move & pull around. Every time I hear move I get sick. Oh! I can't tell you how I feel about everything. I can't get no work, I don't have any clothes or money, I have this old city food. I can't get up with my rent. I am so heart sick with every thing. I wish I was at the poor farm. I am alone all the time, lonely and every thing. I am not well either so I just don't know anything to do.

I don't want to write you as you say everything here is so messed up. There's nothing to write pleasant, so I hate to write at all.

I've only one thing I want to live for and I do want to see you again, but I don't know what will happen to me. You are going to stay away so long. Oh! Langston, if you only could come back, just come nearer may be I could see you some way. Don't bother about me just try to help Gwyn. He's young and must help himself. I don't care I just as leave go to the county farm—for I can't go on [like] this. I just can't. If I leave this house I'll pack your books and ask George to keep them for you. I could not take them to the county home. But if I don't have some thing happen I'll be there next month. But I'll be O.K. It's the only place for poor, old people to be.

Much love,
Mamma.

Oberlin, Ohio
June 7th [1935]

My Dear Son—

Got your letter a few days ago, and found me quite ill, but better today. Thus it is with my ailment unless I have an operation, I guess.

Gwyn was very worried about my state of health, and still is. He is very kind to me and does all he can for my comfort not to be making hardly any wages. When I wrote him I had notice to get out & I had nothing to stay with not nothing to go with. So I could do neither one—go or stay and Gwyn was worried nearly crazy. I was going on out to the Poor farm & end it all. Langston I'm not well and I can't stand any more than I have been through. It's just fate. I don't blame any one, only myself for no one has a right to be dependent on any one at all. So I blame no one. Surely I told him I got the money when it came. I payd 2 month ½ rent still leaving this month. Paid Gas Bill, light Bill, some on 5.00 Gwyn got for uniform and gave him 2.00. I had about $2.00 also for medicine.

Hope you come up to Detroit also over here. I have nothing at all to offer you but such as I have I will be glad to see you.

It is a rainy nasty day and I am here day and night alone save for a little kitten. Now I got to go get me some eats. Gwyn sent me $1.00 last night and I got me a small (very small) chicken for 35¢ & quart of milk so must get me a swell dinner.

One of my friends—my best—had the club to which I belong, so she gave me my supper. She is so nice to me her name is Sadie Whiteside, she used to feed Gwyn, when I was in N.Y. She has one son who is an artist. I want you to see his work. She has another son in Long Island. She lost her mother 2 months ago and she has her big home alone. She used to be Geo. Freeman's (our cousin) Girl, but they fell out over a "sixteener," so no more now. You will enjoy George. He cussed everything and every body but he is good hearted. He & Gwyn don't hit if off at all. But they are both to much alike I guess. You may like Georgie, if not you will like her little Girl Inetia. She is awfully smart. Sings, dances & is just bright. You'll like her. Sorry my dear neighbors next door will be gone when you get here. They are an old, very old couple and I spend much time with them but they go up to Chautauqua June 12 and I will miss them so. It seems I have some protection when they are at home. But I'm not afraid any way any more.

Well, so I pray for you nightly. The other day three weeks ago a new man was preaching here and he said a certain negro writer a poet says "there is no Christ" &ct & I told him. It was real funny, he was talking of you. Well if you can send this month rent & Gas & Light. My water is to be cut off. But I don't care. Hope to see you. We have cousins in Detroit want to know where you'll speak.
Mamma

Oberlin Ohio
June 10th

Dear Langston

Your letter just rec'd. It is all right to send your stuff here And I will be here until I can do something. I owe the rent, the gas & light. Now if you can't send me any money I don't know what to say for I have only 11 cents. Gas & light & water due today. Langston if I had not come here to be with Gwyn as you thought best—God knows I would not be in this mess. Now

I can't work & there's no place but the Poor farm. I spoke for the Federations of Clubs in Eleyria [Elyria] and they were enthused so they invited me to be Guest Speaker at their Annual Convention in Cincinnati June 24th with expenses paid, but I'd have to have a dress—& shoes. Oh, God, why do I have to suffer & never have nothing. Where is the ½ of the Estate you were going to send me?

Now if you can't send me the rent &ct I am again at the place I can't go and I can't stay. God knows if I ever get out of this mess either dead or alive I will have nothing to say—to no *one ever* about money.

Yours
Carolyn

———————

To: (Air Mail)
        Mr. Langston Hughes
        10310 Weigand Ave
        Los Angeles, Calif.
        Tell me where to write

Oberlin Ohio
June 12 [1935]

Dear Langston

I am just trying to ans. Your last letter. Just rec'd. Thanks for the fiver. It will pay gas & water rent. I am only worried about the rent for I want this place until you get here anyway. We then will talk over matters. I was getting along fine and my Dr. died. Well now I will have to try to get another one on the relief.[1] The tumor is still here but seems much better.

Well, Langston I've hope and prayed for your return. I will be so happy. It cost very little to live here if one every gets straight, but I was in debt. Now I hope to get all O.K. so I can live cheaply if I stay.

I am so lonely. I don't know.

Langston, are you going to N.Y. or what. Or coming from Detroit here. We have cousins there and they want to know where you will speak & all about it. So let me know at once. Do you want a date here? I have plenty to eat but have gas, light, water and medicine to buy. And I have no clothes at all. Am invited as a guest speaker at State Federation at Cincy June 24th But no clothes.

Now I can answer all these questions? I hope I will get over so much worry. I hate to be all worried to death cross & sick too.

Got a nice letter from Gwyn he send me $7.00 & anything he has to spare. Great Boy Gwyn is.

Much love & write soon. Mother is anxious to know when you will come.

Mamma.

1. After the death of the doctor who treats the "blood tumor" on her breast with "hypodermics," Carrie finally sees a doctor in a public health clinic who abruptly and brutally, without any preparation, tells her she has breast cancer. She refuses to go to "charity" doctors again because they "talk to people like dogs" and she refuses the surgery that the doctor recommended. She does submit to a series of external beam radiation or "X-ray" treatments. Early radiation therapy worked by killing the fastest-growing cells, the cancer cells, but also "burned" the skin in the process. Treatment methods that were not as destructive to skin tissue were developed in the late 1960s and have continued to progress so that tumors are isolated and irradiated with little damage to healthy tissue.

―――――――――

100 Kisses

[Letterhead] Langston Hughes
2256 East 86th Street
Cleveland, Ohio
July 14th [1935]

My Dearest Boy:

Just got your letter written on the ship. I was so very glad to hear. I have waited and counted the days. It is very hot here and Gwyn has walked him self sick trying to get a job but he's only got his camp job. He has worked about six days altogether.

I am so glad you are all o.k. and safe. We are moving out to Bessie's Sat and Kit leaves for Camp[1] about 4.30 Sat eve. I wish he could have made some money. But the camp break will net him about $32.00 so that will be something. Your stuff is all packed and labeled from each drawer and all. Nothing messed up. I did it all. So carefully I packed & sealed it. So not one paper is lost or strayed. All you have to do is unseal each box, marked & find any thing you want. You will see how Darling *much love*. Write as often as you can as it takes so long.

Much love to you. Yours lovingly
Your Mother.

Ruby has a Job. So has Jaine so it is very quiet around here. Old Blunt is so afraid I won't move or pay him every penny he is here every minute nearly. Black Imp.

Mason is out of a job and could not even pay room rent yet. Well, I feel sorry for him because they have not paid him yet. Julia has been here today. She says you must accept her kiss & hug. I went to exposition with a couple from N.Y. Irene can stop with me very nicely.

1. Gwyn is going to the Civilian Conservation Corps camp in Elyria, Ohio.

———————————

Write soon ["soon" double-underlined]

[circa July 15, 1935]
Oberlin Ohio
58 E Vine

Dearest Boy:—I am still here, but cannot remain here but two weeks. The old lady says "we must move." After I paid her $24.50 then she writes she wants the house, so that's that. That is Gwyn's fault, for she hated him & is bound to break all connections between us. All well & good. Now also Gwyn has a terrible cold, lost his job and has been home all week. So now I am in a situation I don't know what to do. If I could find another place here I'd love it. But there is only large houses & I can't afford them and then one can't make any income on anything here. I have very few pieces of furniture also now. I can stay here until Aug 2th. I hope you could come by then and maybe we could do something—if you stay with us.

I was at the convention of the Federation of Clubs of Women, about

3000 women. And your dear friend Mrs. Bethune, hopped up and told the convention that the dear little poet, Langston Hughes, had a mother in the audience and I was clapped up there. Was I excited. She is crazy over you. I saw & talked to Mr. & Mrs. Napier, he is so feeble, But very lovely. They talked and exploded your Virtues. Now Gwyn wants to go there to School & work his way through. I talked long to Mrs. Mary Church Terrell,[1] and a family from Miss. who knew you, Mr. & Mrs. Ross.

All the southern "mammas" were so please to see me. They all remembered you.

Now the problem, is what and where and when, If I am to have Gwyn. I don't know where to stay. He must work some. He can't get it here. It's a terrible problem to know what to do for the best.

But Langston, I do want to see you and I wanted you to come while I felt fairly well. For this tumor gets no better and I am getting worried about it. If you can I wish you could come home.

Did you ever get the [Guggenheim] Award? I never heard you say what you intended to do with it. Bessie—you know Brown went out home to Kansas this week. It made me home sick. Auntie Reed is very feeble. The fare out there from here is $26.00 round trip, I think.

The fare on both bus and train is greatly decreased. Bessie went on train and it only cost her $41.00 round trip rate.

Let me know the names of your child's book please. Gwyn has gone back over to Cleveland tonight. He will be back Sunday night. If I had the old lady who owns this house I'd spank her good. She is the old Scratch, don't know what to do for meanness. Oh well. Something will turn up and It will be O.K. *Your* [double-underlined] manuscripts are here from *Mexico* [double-underlined]. I told you two or three times. Send your things here if you want. We'll keep them with us somewhere.

Mother Carolyn

1. An educator and civil rights leader, Mary Church Terrell (1863–1954) was arguably the most influential Black woman in Washington.

Oberlin, Ohio
July 27 [1935]

Dear Langston,

I am sorry that I have to write you with pencil, but I wanted you to get it at once. You remember the place I lived last year 117 S Main St. Well the man has fell on it so he got a government loan on it for $2,200 and is to pay $18 per month. He has made up payments leaving $2,128 to pay. Now since I rented a year from him, he just came to see me, offered me the place for $100 cash & take up the loan of $18 per month. Now the house is a double house. 4 rooms both up stairs, 9 rooms down. Hardwood floors and the whole place is in good condition. Has a double lot, fruit of all kinds basement that will rent also. The down stairs rents for $13 to $17 per month. There were never any colored people lived in it but us. It is a nice place and right on the street (that is the principal street). Would you consider it—I thought if you wanted a home here was a cheap chance. Four years ago the house sold for $6,000. White neighborhood entirely. Let me know from you at once. If you are interested.

Mother

Langston I am so enthused over the idea, if we only could you & Gwyn would always have a nice home. We could rent it all until we paid for it. We could [do] that maybe in three years.

———————

[August 4, 1935]
Oberlin Ohio
58 E Vine

Kit chloroformed our cat today.

My Darling Boy: Oh I just want to see you worse than anything I know of *now* [double-underlined]. Sat. eve and I am alone and Oh! I do want to see you. Your special came this a.m. I heard the bell, called Gwyn and he run down and got it. The owner came after noon, he is anxious to sell as he has such miserable luck this year he says he can't stay here any longer.

He once was a wealthy man. You should see him now. Now first I want to answer all your questions.

The loan from the Government was procured on the property about four months ago, before the loan is give[n] all back taxes have to be paid on. They take them out of the loan therefore there is no taxes until June 1936. The down stairs is rented now but if Negroes get it, but I know of some one whom I think will take it Colored. Perhaps we could rent it all for a year, then live in it then.[1] We would have it half paid for. The title is clear, according to the Government loan, as reliable people told me there be no government loan with out clear title. We can get lots of cheaper places, so if we wait until you come we can look them over. One little place with six rooms sold for $435. Property is dirt cheap here. But this is a white place white neighborhood. Will sell again readily Because white people don't want Negro neighbors & the place has four rentable compartments. Upstairs, first floor, basement, small apartment of 2 rooms in rear. But when you come we will look if you are still in the notion, if this one is gone. We may even do better. I hope you will be here before Aug 15th as we have to give up this house and as yet I have no other, but if you can come I'll stay here until we can get settled.

Please read all this letter. There is only two vacant houses here. One 12— one 15. So Darling come on home soon as you come you know. It seems so long since I have seen you. And I am not so well at all.

Mrs. Bethune was lovely. Had a leter from Auntie Reedie wants me to come out there. I'd love to stay a month or so out there. Bus fare $21.00 round trip. It is apt to be cheaper. Kit is here. Unsatisfied has no work, want to go to Camp now. I think it would make a man of him.

Write soon

Mamma

1. This is a business tactic Carrie surely learned from her mother, who would rent out her house in Lawrence, Kansas, to college students and move herself and Langston to her friends' home for the year.

[October 1935]

If not to Cleveland I will come to N.Y. or what can be done

Dear Lang:

Was very glad to hear about your play, hope that it will be a grand slam. I thought sure that you would be home by now. I wish that you had of been here to buy me a coat today at May cos. Coats & suits for $11 a piece. Two for the price of one. Boy it sure has been cold here for the last two days. We have a stove and it sure feels good. Are you coming home on your way West? College plays Rochester today. This I see it from over fence. Bring home a fifth of Gin. Tell all hellow.

Dear Langston,

I am very proud to hear of your success of the Play.[1] I hope that it will run longer than our play then you will have made some money. I am just remembering where the letters are.

I went to the Dr. and he tried to scare me to death and almost succeeded.[2] I have been sick every since. Well, I have to go to Cleveland see if I can get some treatments, if not its all over. Well, what's the use to worry we have to die with something.

I had to buy a stove, had to pay rent, two gas and light bill and the other things, and Gwyn got no pay at all yet, so I have no money and I want to go to Cleveland soon as I can.

So if you are not coming home at once send me a little so I can go over there and get the verdict I am ill today and have been all week just nervous over what the Dr. said, and I am no worse off yet.

Well let us know what you are going to do. Love to all. Hope you are very happy. Kisses for you.

1. Here Carrie applauds Langston for his *Mulatto*, which opened October 24, 1935, at the Vanderbilt Theatre in New York City.

2. Langston received a letter dated October 23, 1935, from Stanley E. Brown, M.D. Physician and Surgeon, 4001 Central Avenue, Room 9, Cleveland, Ohio: "Dear Langston: It is with much [sorrow] that I must inform you that your mother has a far advanced cancer of the breast. I referred her to Dr. Holloway, a surgeon at Lakeside. This treatment is only palliative, and may prolong life. I thought it best not to inform your mother of the serious-

ness of her disease. We encouraged her as much as possible. Wishing you the best of health. I am Sincerely yours, Stanley E. Brown." He also enclosed a bill with a note: "Your mother requested that I send you her bill. SEB." The bill was for four dollars.

———————————

[Typed letter]
Oberlin, Ohio
Oct. 26, 1935

Dear Langston:

Your letter came to us this morning and as you know we all were anxious to see the result of the First Nighter, and I think that the kind of play it was, and knowing white people as we do, they did well on their write ups, for way down in any of their hearts, they do not want that sort of thing brought before their very eyes and I am sure that a many one burned to see the truth there on Broadway, so I really think the papers did very well, as they are all white and all predjuce, and they at least gave you credit for the work and your feelings.

So I am very happy over it all. I read and reread them over and over and I feel they were very good, considering the writers.

Well, I guess that Gwyn is really leaving, as he told the Captain he wanted to get a discharge as he was to take a job in N.Y. and the Captain said that if he could do so and go to school that he would give him an honorable discharge, if I write a letter to that effect, and Gwyn says he means to go to Night School.

It seems that his trip to N.Y. has more than anything woke him up to the fact that he must finish school, as he cannot do anything much without it, he seem to feel the responsibility more today.

I guess he will leave the first, and I do hope he can get a job and get settled for at least a year or so. He must find himself soon, and quit stalling around, and get a start at something.

As for me, I am in your hands, and what ever you think best I will willingly do, for I do not want to cause you one moment's worry. I can do anything it will be alright, as do not care either way.

I knew that this tumor had not grown any in a year, and that it could not be so bad yet, as I have no bad effects yet. I believe that if Dr. Brown had not known you and thought you had money I could have gotten free Clinic treatments, but he said it would never do for me, being your mother, to go to the Clinic.

Now you think it all over and when you come we will talk it over and the best and especially the cheapest thing to do, we will do. But I do not want you to worry constantly about me. You have your own life to live and I will not be one to hamper it. I have lived to see you both grown, and do not need me at all so, why let you worry and spend on me. I can live in one little room anywhere, and if I get well I can work. If not, all well and good.

Now I am hoping that your Play will go on and on, and that you will have nothing but success forever, and I do love you so much. I feel so greatful to you for all you have done for me.

We could all have stayed as no one was looking for them till on Sunday, were we mad. But I had such a nice time and every one was kind to us and we certainly had a fine time and Sadie and Opal felt you treated them so nicely that they will never forget it.

Well. Now I have said it all. I have [hope] that you will consider all I have said and do the cheapest thing for you and any plans you make will be all right with me.

Yours Lovingly,
Mother

I realize Gwyn also is a man & wants to go for himself and I can't hinder him either. If possible I'd like to be near you all or near some one near to me if not o.k.

———

Oberlin, Ohio
Nov 11th [1935]

Darling Boy—

I am so sorry about Sallie. I felt so bad about it. It completely broke me up for this week.[1] I got a letter from Bessie this A.M. and she invited you to stop with her & Charley. And Mr. Ramey wanted to know when you arrived so the teachers could meet you.

I will bring your books down. They came today. Gwyn never got his money yet from the camp. We were very disappointed because you could not come home but I am glad you could go to Indianapolis on account of your Uncle John. You better send me 2.00, the books are 81¢. Only have about one dollar for I fear Gwyn won't get his money. Thanks.

Bessie Address—

> 10520 Englewood Ave
> Cleveland, Ohio.

It will be so nice to see you again for I am always waiting to see you.

It is getting cold today and radio says very cold tonight. We have no coal but will try to get a little. Gwyn has tried to get ready to go to N. Y. but he has had no money nor I either so he is still here. I sure hope he gets work there and settles to try to go to Night School. Now hoping to see you soon.

Yours Lovingly—
Mother
Regards to John.

Am mailing one cutter also[2]

---

1. Sallie Garvin, James Nathaniel Hughes's sister, died from breast cancer in 1935 after a mastectomy and other treatments. Carrie's sorrow can also be read as an admission of fear about a possible similar outcome that awaits her.

2. In conversation with the editors, Allison Smith, chair of the Art History Department at Johnson County Community College, defined a "cutter," "block cutter," or "wood cut" this way: "A type of relief print in which a wooden block is carved to create a scene or design. The background of the scene is carved away resulting in blank (white) space on the paper, while the area to be printed is a raised surface holding the applied ink."

Thursday
Cleveland Ohio
Nov 26th [1935]

My Dear Dear Boy:—

Your post card letter came to me today and I was very very glad to hear from you. It seems you don't have time to write me at all and I feel so lonely just to hear from you. So sorry you can't be with your "family" on Thanksgiving, we all wanted you so much. Had you come we would have had a turkey, but now I think we will be satisfied with a little chicken. Well, Gwyn stays up to Mrs. Marck's all together. She is crazy about Gwyn.

I wrote to Toy and she never answered, at all. I may not have the right number is it 102 E. 127 st. Apt 2E—Am I wrong? If so send me the number please.

I met a Mrs. Hill-Williams from New York yesterday and she wrote the "Fairy Four Leaf Clover" and she has had it published and the two plays in it played at some college. Do you know her. She is also the neice of Pres. Johnson of Lincoln College. Do you know her. You just met her Aunt at Lincoln University last time you were there. When she saw me she bowed very profoundly to me saying "Langston Hughes Mother, that great great boy. I bow to you."

Enclosed find one $5.00 the last I have on the books. Will send so you can sport Thanksgiving anyway. I was quite ill this week for three days some stomach trouble also. Just tried to eat. Am better now also.

Dearest I'd love to see you. *Have* [triple-underlined] to seems so *long*. You have dozens of invitations to read here. *Why not.*

Yours,
Mamma

———————

[Dec 25, 1935]

My Dearest Boy—

At home all safe and sound, sleepy.

Oh! Baby, I am with you tonight hoping & praying for your play. Your own child—your own production. Oh! I hope it goes all o.k.

Heard from Doctors. Say operation is best, but its slow growing tumors. When you come we will see them and make arrangements.

Love and all. Thanks for all you done. Yours.

Love to Toy and Emmerson. Will write them.

Mamma

All gang says thanks and will write you—

———————

Dec. 26 [1935]
Oberlin, Ohio
58 E. Vine

My Dear Son—

The day after Xmas and I worked yesterday and on Xmas eve, so today I am all in. But I was so glad to make the little money. It was great to get the telegram after all you've done. I am not worthy of half your sweetness. I am just an old cranky worrying soul. No good to anyone much. But I am so proud of you and so fond of you. You are my very life. I know no interest scarcely out side of you and how you are and how you get on and all. I know you are so very lovely to me, but Langston it hurts to take for I don't want to deprive you of what you need.

The year is only a few days from closing and I am just thinking that one year ago, I was well & working. Now I am hurt, not much good, no work or money. No good. I got cards from Mae Perk & Mother. Also Auntie Reed. She is still getting younger. Heard also from Lotta. I also saw Netting Langston of Washington D.C. Xmas week. She looks fine has work in Chicago. Her children are large nearly grown up. Nettie Harlan oldest boy is married and has a baby over which they all rave. Have not heard one word from Homer. I saw Erma & Lou first time in three years. You knew the old lady Mac passed on. You remember "Mamma lost. Some one took Mamma." Dear old lady is through moving here & there. Now Langston as it is the new year nearly I want you to know how we stand to start out. I have pinched, saved, done all I could but can't have anything. Now Coal is the worse item to get hold of it is so high & last so little time.

Please read this over so you will see how things are for us—

Rent	$8.00	December
Gas Bill	2.85	
Light Bill	1.00	
Coal 1 ton monthly	5.00	
Groceries	5.00	
	$21.85	

Now that's eating little cheap food and being very saving with fuel.

Debts we *owe.*

Gwyn's suit	$13.00
(I pay some every month)	
For moving	$2.00
Cod liver oil for Gwyn *2 bottles*	$3.00

And Gwyn takes money to go to Richmond to see Bettie! Now Langston I do all I can: save and stint. My clothes are all worn out but I don't care for that so I can do as you wish me to. This little house is very old. I want to get a closed in place. No doors here downstairs. I wanted you to see this statement so you knew how we stood on the first of the year to start out.

I am sorry I am such a pest and such a burden. But if ever I work I won't be. Xmas I worked all day. I was glad in the evening I went to a lady for dinner Then house to make a fire and in for eve. It was very dull around here. Amele & Pet went to the Cotton Club in Cleveland.

Now I hope you see just how I stand and everything will be clear to you. I have $11.00 left out of the Xmas fund.

Love Happy New Year.

Mother

Dear Lovely Death
1936–1938

Fascination with death properly belongs also to Langston—a number of his poems from this period reflect grief, loneliness, pathos, and melancholy—but after Carrie's discovery of the "blood tumor" on her breast, a subtle shift of tone in the extant letters of this three-year period hints at her awareness of mortality. She appears to be less demanding, acerbic, and manipulative in seeking fusion with others in order to meet her own needs and wants. Her outward expression of concern, especially to Langston and Gwyn, is often businesslike as she reports on the progress of her own health. When her inner feelings make it onto paper, she is less willing to blame others and more likely to assume responsibility for her life. It is as if she has come to accept that her life now hung in the balance and that no one could alter the inevitable outcome. Only a comparatively few letters make up this oeuvre in contrast to the flurry of writing she undertook in 1935. Whether writing in a rather dispassionate manner or a confessional mode, she generally sees the end of her life as a fait accompli. In a March 8, 1936, letter, she writes: "I'm dying, I think."

The unfolding narrative of the treatments she undergoes for her cancer is especially interesting for its relative absence of self-pity. Initially, she details the amount of money the treatments will cost, the fare to travel back and forth to the hospital, and other logistical details. Her physician, Dr. Holloway, starts her off with what she describes as "Electric treatments" performed by the X-ray department, at a cost of fifteen dollars for twelve treatments. No doubt her spirits are buoyed by the doctor's optimism that the tumor has already shrunk a bit, thus requiring fewer treatments. Even when the estimated number of treatments is increased from eighteen to thirty, she has reason to be hopeful and asserts, "I am getting better." Her feelings are undoubtedly sorely tested when Dr. Stanley Brown, at Langston's request, goes to Carrie's apartment to check up on her. He immediately prescribes medication and tries to persuade her to enter a hospital. Carrie resists, saying that her doctor, in this case one named Friedman, has not issued the orders, and so she feels compelled to ignore Brown's assumption of her care. Brown goes so far as to say that he is working with the agreement of Carrie's landlady, disclosing that Carrie has "an incurable disease" and saying that she should not be allowed to remain at home. The nearly hysterical Carrie rebuts Brown's diagnosis and contests her impending eviction by a landlady who fears her cancer, alleging that Dr. Friedman is adamant in saying "No one knows her condition but me and she *is cured.*"

Even her smothering of Gwyn, her over-involvement, takes a turn in these letters. While she still frets about her capricious, immature stepson, the worry is less intense, as if she has finally decided to let go and let him learn about life on his own. When he manages to enroll in a program at Wilberforce College, she writes Langston: "About Wilberforce, if you cannot don't bother. For I know what it is to be without money." She knows all too well the poor academic record Gwyn has established. Instead of pouring good money after bad, she advises Langston to put his hard-earned funds to better use. The change in attitude is truly remarkable since Carrie herself rarely said no to Gwyn. She misses the irony when mildly chastising Langston for attending too much to Gwyn's needs: "Kit wants to [*sic*] much and you always do it instead of saying 'No' some time." In her weakened condition, she has probably forgotten that he mainly provides for Gwyn because of her nagging insistence.

She admits to worrying, but a great deal of it focuses on Langston, not Gwyn. During Langston's brief period in Spain, where he reports on the civil war for the *Baltimore Afro-American*, she is consumed with fear for Langston's life. The letters they exchange are received sporadically, at best, and this inability to communicate regularly pushes Carrie to the emotional edge: "I went to pieces, had hysterics." What makes this emotional response so different from previous ones is that money ceases to be at the center of her feelings. She seems sincerely interested in his well-being. Similarly, Carrie's periodic admission to being lonely is more an unburdening of her soul rather than pathos designed to elicit self-serving attention. In nearly every instance of her entering this confessional mode, her statements are casually interjected between business-related or mundane family matters. There they do not call attention to themselves.

The image of Carrie that emerges from these letters, then, is of someone chastened, humbled, and resigned. After failing to secure an apartment she really wants, she writes to Langston: "It was alright to me for I can stay here until Shiloh comes." This is one of the first times she virtually announces that her end is near. Later, in the same letter, she states that she has six months to live. As if to deflect attention away from the pathos of this admission and therefore from herself, she turns to news about St. James Church burning down and the Gilpin Players performing Rudolph Fisher's plays. Then, as if engaged in full disclosure about her current condition, she writes: "My arm is almost so I can't use it at all any more." Carrie is resigned to her fate.

Cleveland Ohio
Jan 20th [1936]

My Dear Boy:

The Plain Dealer[1] reporter has been calling me for a month & been out here. Wants to get in touch with you. I gave him your address tonight. The Afro American send you a check for $50.00 and I put it in the bank to. I am sending you the slip for the same. It was on your saving account.

$50.00	from	Afro
27.50	" "	American Society of Composers
5.69	" "	HollyWood Production of "Soul gone home."
———		
83.19		

None of this was on your checking account. Then I put one more $27.50 from American S. C. Maybe two I can't remember. Then some one else deposited $10.50 cents and another I think for $22.20. I do not know who sent that.

Well I am sending this to you by air mail—

I am also sending some of your letters also. You should see your book "Not Without Laughter," published in Shanghi. It is the most comical looking book, with your picture on the back or front.

I want to say so much to you I can't think of it. When you left us in July I have all the bank accounts. Here they are so you will understand.

Elmer got in "Who's Who" art book. He is the only Negro.

1. The Cleveland, Ohio, daily newspaper.

———————

Did you hear from Plaindealer?

Cleveland Ohio
Jany 24

My Dear Son,

I hope you got your things. I got the sore throat and neuritis. Don't feel very well today. I went out to the hospital with Raynor yesterday. It was lovely day but damp. He says when are you coming home? Now listen carefully. *I am going to move.* I have been here since August. I have had to carry all water up stairs, sick or well. I have no bathroom and they put a bell on the back door for *my* [double-underlined] company. So of course I would not use it. Why my company at the back? So everything here is inconvenient. No sink. No bath room. No convenience and car fare from here is to high & I am paying $20.00 for this. Now I have got a apartment with 4 room, one for you off from us all. Where you can shut the door & work. All this is $17.00 per month. And *Pay for gas.* Large gas stove. Lovely little reception room. Wash room outside, place for chatting to have you'll like it I know the people were lovely. Gwyn hates out here & I don't get along with any of them folks here for they have talked lots about him, just little tack things and has made us all suffer and unhappy. Now answer at once. Tell me to move because I want a nice place when you come. Please come soon as you can come. I am sending you list of how I have used the money. Yours waiting to see you so bad.

Mamma

Cleveland

Dearest: I forgot to tell you that when you are in Raleigh that you are in my Mother's birthday place and they say the old Brick plant and home of your great grandfather Patterson is still there. See about it. Ask for Leary's Chesttnutts, Ockeltrees, Waldrons. I sent this air mail to tell you of the fact. Also go to Fayette if you can. Langston all the Libraries want to know where is the Child's Book. I hope you get this.

Pet is finishing Physiology at Western Reserve out this year with a Ph.D. & B.A. She says her Prof only name you as the poet worthy of study. Isn't that great.—Mama

---

[1936]
Clark Hotel[1] [letterhead]
1820–24 So. CENTRAL AVENUE
Washington Blvd. & Central Ave.
Los Angeles, CALIF
Saturday eve.

Dear Langston,

Just got your letter. I have almost decided on a place. But I must go to the hospital Monday at 12. For if not fear I can't get in on this place that Dr. Holloway[2] fixed for me. Special. I must have a little money by Monday for I don't know how I will be, will need some. (over) [circled] I have been quite sick.

(Will arrange about Mail sure). So send me something to Amelia's by Monday (Special) there after the trip to the Hospital will write you every thing and you will know just how I am and how I will be "fixed up" and what I have to have. Send me $5.00 at least by Monday. Then I will write you tell you everything. How long I will be there. How much I will have to pay, room rent and all. How often I will take treatments. I do not know anything now. Will expect to hear from you at Amelia's Monday A.M.

Yours lovingly,
Mother

Guess you got this telegram anyway.
2245 E. 80th.

Mamma

1. Langston's favorite hotel in Los Angeles, California. He was quite possibly drawn to the hotel's dollar-a-day rate. He must have brought Carrie a supply of their letterhead stationery. She had not been to Los Angeles.

2. Reconstructing the precise order of the doctors who provide Carrie medical care after the discovery of the "blood tumor" on her breast is challenging, since the extant records are few. Beginning May 14, 1935, when she writes Langston about her condition, Carrie sees a number of doctors, some of whom can be identified and others not. Her initial physician, whom she describes as a "charity" doctor, treats her with "hypodermics." Although she refuses surgery, she does consent to a series of "external beam radiation" or X-ray treatments. The death of this first physician forces her to seek care from a provider in a public health clinic. This one "scares her to death," forcing her to seek money from Langston to locate a

"private" doctor. Langston responds by dispatching Dr. Stanley E. Brown to examine her. Brown writes Langston that she has "advanced cancer" and refers her to Dr. Holloway, a surgeon at Lakeside Hospital in Cleveland, for palliative care. By Christmas Day 1935, she learns that she has "slow growing tumors." In January 1936, Dr. Holloway convinces her to enter a hospital for a series of "electric treatments." Despite being told that the tumor has been reduced, the number of treatments is increased from eighteen to thirty. In February and March 1936, the number of treatments increased the severity of the damaging effects on Carrie's body, prompting Dr. Brown to make several house calls. Carrie blames Brown for her apparently worsening condition. At one point, when he seeks to hospitalize Carrie, she responds angrily to his proposal and to his prescription for sleeping pills. Her reaction is probably exacerbated by his revelation to her that she has "an incurable disease," which prompts her landlady to try to evict Carrie. Carrie insists that "her doctor," Dr. Friedman, be called. (She consistently misspells his name as "Freedman.") Paradoxically, he convinces her to go to the hospital even though he reassures her that she's getting better. In her March 8, 1936, letter to Langston, she reports Friedman's rebuke of Brown: "No one knows her condition but me and she is cured." She is far from escaping the ravages of her cancer. In a March 10, 1938, letter, Dr. Charles Herbert Garvin reveals to Langston that he has received X-rays of Carrie from Dr. Friedman that show that the cancer has metastasized into her lungs. A month later the doctors dismiss her from the hospital. Two months later she loses her valiant fight to live.

[1936]
[On Clark Hotel letterhead]

Have not heard of Gwyn at all.

** rents are high here. Think I will perhaps not move until warmer weather. So cold to break up.

Cleveland, Ohio
2245 E. 80th

Dearest:

I just got your letter. I am feeling fair seem to be standing the treatment very fair. But today got held up by 2 confidence men and was scared so bad that I have been almost ill all day. It was when I was coming from the hospital. Of course they got nothing. I only had 15 cents, but it scared me out of six weeks growth. I got your money this P.M. I will pay part of it to the hospital, then pay one week's room rent again. I eat very cheaply also here, so most times 30 cents per day. I will also get a street car pass—it is much cheaper. My expenses is $15.00 for 12 treatments

1.25	pass
2.50	room
2.00	board

This week $20.75

Then I had to get a pair of rubbers, peroxide, gauze, & etc. But I am sorry if you think it is too much for I can stop them, though they think it is helping the place. I must get Gwyn some thing to eat this week for eats were low when I left. It is awful cold here but the Phyllis[1] is awful warm. I am very comfortable here. Let me know if it's too much.

Yours
Mamma

1. The Phillis Wheatley house.

Wednesday–Tuesday [*sic*]

Dear Langston—

I just got back tonight. So am sending your mail at once. Could not see the Dr. until Tuesday and was ill all the time I was there.

Dr. Holloway wants me to begin Electric treatments at once. Will cost nothing and he will supervise them. Says the place is down so now it can be healed. He wants me to take the first one Monday 12:45. Only have a room and stay in the city.

Gwyn came back with me. [in margin on side]

Hope you are o.k.

Let me hear at once.

Mother C——

Cleveland Ohio
Monday

Dear Langston:

I just got back from the Hospital. I will now tell you all I need. I am going to stay at the Phillys Wheatley. I will get a room at the Phyllys for $2.50 per week. Then I will go out ever day for a treatment. A pass will cost me $1.25 per week and the treatments will be $15.00—12 X Ray. I may not need the 12 but must pay the $15.00. Now you see just what I need for the two weeks—minus eating. Then they say I will be well of this. I had numerous Drs. All say the same thing. That it has reduced so until it will only take a few treatments. Now send the money at once by Thursday any way. I have to start treatments at once. Send to Amelia's please.

Gwyn is in Oberlin. He has had an awful cold. I was sick also three days am better now. Now Langston, you wanted this done. Dr. said out of the clinic, it would cost me $100.00 so you see what we saved. Hoping to hear from you at once. Dearie, I hope you this will be all right to you and you can do this.

Hoping for your Letter by return mail. I am your anxiously

Mother—

P.S. I arranged about your mail. No more has come for you.

———————

I HAD DINNER WITH Bess & Charley on Sunday and they were fine. I saw Amelie. She cut these clippings for you also.

Cleveland, Ohio
Jany 27th [1936]

Dearest

I just got in from the hospital and they had a consultation about me and they have decided that the 12 treatments must be increased to 18 more, now that means one month treatment. Just as I thought it would be when I started. Now I paid $8.00 out of the $20.00 at the Hospital. I bought a pass $1.25. I paid $2.50 room rent. I gave Gwyn $1.30 and I have been eating with the rest. I also had to buy myself a sweater as my coat is so thin and its been 10°, 8–7 degrees below. It's been so cold and I've had to go the Hospital. Each day any way. Now for the other 18 treatments they will only charge me $10.00 making the whole bill $25.00. But the great trouble is, I have to stay right here. Each and every day. I must be here. And its been so cold. I could find no place as after the treatment I lie down. Most of the time. Now if I take the rest, I will have to pay $16.00 dollars more at the Hospital. 2 weeks more rent. 2 more passes. And eats. Now if you think you can do this I will have to let the X-Ray department know by Saturday. For if I don't stay in they give some one else my place in the clinic. Now Darling, don't try to do what you cannot now. I am only telling you. Count it up and see what the bill will be.

Hospital Bill	$16.00
Car Fare	2.50
Room Rent	5.00
Eating *about* [double-underlined]	
40¢ per day—2 weeks	5.60
	————
From Jany 27–Feby 10th 1936	*$29.10*

I have to pay the last $10 Feby 2nd. Gwyn came up with Mrs. Bell Sat. eve & had dinner with me and went back. He said he was doing fairly well. Hope you are fine. Much love.

Answer soon

Yours,

Mamma

So I see they barred you from Gary but Gary ain't much any way so why worry about them. Miss Margaret DeWitt at the play house wish to know will you be here for the Negro Congress next month?

————————

Western Union Telegram

January 29, 1936

LANGSTON HUGHES = CARE ARNA BONTEMPS 731 EAST 50 PL
APT=

WILL LOSE PLACE HOSPITAL MUST HAVE MONEY IN
MORNING ANSWER IMMEDIATELY BY WESTERNUNION=

MOTHER

———————

Jany 30 [1936]

My Dear Son:

So sorry I sent the telegram but I was worried. I hated to give up the place. As if you cannot continue, your place is taken, so you are out and on and on. But its all o.k. thanks and I am sorry I had to worry you.

Gwyn was up for his girl's school finish. He hunted for work all around while here went to see Welfare Workers &ct.

I can get an apartment here for $13.00 per month. Mrs. Cooper's place & Amele says she will pay $4.00 for her brother per week to stay with us.

What do you think and Gwyn says he will get moved up. Of course until the treatments are over, I can't do much towards moving, but I packed most of my things and he says he can do the rest. But of course we can't do anything just now. I hope after this place is healed I can get a little job and help myself. Perhaps pay you back for part you've done. I am sorry and feel it is a shame that everything has devolved on you so. Oh! If I could only help *my* self. Yet it's too bad. Thus so I had to do for my poor dear mother but hoped never to have to depend on someone else. Thanks a thousand times. Gwyn got coal from charity at home. See your name up today to address Negro Youth Congress. Bessie says if they will only take Elanor I can have her room. They have a car now. My whole bill at Hospital was $25.00. I have over half paid. It was wonderful of Dr. Holloway to get that price for 30 treatments for it is an expensive treatment.

Now Amele & Pet have been wonderful to me. I have had many meals & they ask me daily.

The Phyllys is very nice, warm & cheap and It was very cold for my hospital trips, but it is better now & Pet lent me her heavy coat, so I'm o.k. Much love to you and you are just lovely to me. I can't thank you. But I love & pray for you. Why don't the Show pay now, pray? What excuse?

———————

[Postmark: February 5, 1936]
Cleveland Ohio—Wednesday

Dear Langston: It is very cold today, wind cut like a knife on the trip to Hospital. I am getting better. Please send me two autographed copys of "Not without Laughter." They are cheaper. I want to give them to my Doctor and nurse. They are so love to me, both know of you &ct. I hope you will write soon.

Yours truly,
Mother—

———————

[February 9, 1936]
Cleveland, Ohio
Sunday

Dear Boy

I got your letter yesterday and I was not well all week. The treatments now are becoming quite severe, as they will be for about a week. They are now so close to my body the body is scorched & burned and it is very painful. And yesterday I came in was trying to wash my underware, and the shelf from over the bath bowl being loose, fell and broke on my hand and cut in three places. And it bled so that it possibly cut a vein so now I am bandaged up in the right hand. So I can't write much. Gwyn is here went to see about a job at the Youth's office and has to be here Monday to see about it.

Will be glad to see you. Bessie has lost the girl downstairs. So you can stay there. I have 12 more treatments to take. About moving, I guess it is all right, but I am not able to do one thing now. I must pay Mrs. Baily for at least light and gas. We can get Coopers for $13.00. But if there was only Kit & I we could not keep up that rent, but if Bill comes with us o.k. But as yet he has got no more pension. I will write more when my hand heals.

I am a most unfortunate soul ["most" and "unfortunate" double-underlined].

Love—Yours
Mamma

Cleveland, Ohio
[February 28, 1936]
Friday

Dear Langston

Just got your letter. I had some medicine down to Drug Store. Needed it and did not have quite enough money to get it. Therefore the telegram—

I think I am a little better, but the weather is terrible and I can't get out in either rain or snow and I have been crazy with lonesomeness. Dear, I can't tell you how glad I will be to come to you. Oh! Baby, just to be in the town with you to see you at lease every day or so. And it will be nice to be near Toy. And there is so much there that will keep one from being lonesome. I will try to come as soon as I can get ready. I will have everything pack and leave nothing of yours. The mattresses, Gwyn shaving stand, magazine stand, book case, desk, can just be carried down with the packed things and freighted to N.Y. with little expense. All the things trunk of books and everything else can be freighted up there. That won't be much trouble for anyone. I'll bring some of your things in my trunk, like tuxedo and shirts. What do you mean by Chinese, you meant [books in the] bath room etc.

Yes, I'll bring your books, Chines, Russian, Yiddish, &ct.

I don't think we will have to buy much. I have lots of dishes, some of the cooking things. I'll bring silver, linens. Well Darling, I will be so glad and I will do the best I can, trust me for that.

Now Darling. I hope you are all o.k. and happy. I will start the packing Monday. I could not get ready before next week. Now write when you can. Much love to you, Toy and Emmerson.

Yours,
"Mom"

———————

[March 4, 1936]

Dear Langston Mother's Boy:

Four days I have been very ill but today I am a little better. I went to the hospital. They said I was o.k. but being frail & thin and rundown it went worse with me. But to try hard to build up an in a few weeks I'd be much better. At last we have a place. An old friend of mine. Oh, I am so glad a nice big front room for me a room for Gwyn & light heat & gas *for $14.00 per month Wonderful.* I am so glad over it. Gwyn got a job today also through Mr. Jelliff.[1]

I was surprised to see $10.00. I was o.k. but I had to help Gwyn so after his pay he'll be o.k.

Write soon
Mamma.

We will move Wednesday week. We will be at 2200 E. 70th. Tell me about award and what about your play. I think when you can you can stay with us. We'll be moved in a week.

1. Gwyn had earlier written to Langston, imploring him to send money: "Borrow some money, take some or something, But send her some right away. She is about to be put out of the house and her gas and light will be shut off next week unless she gets some more. It will be very humiliating for her. . . . If you can't send her any I am going to hold up some body maybe the boss, for she has got to have some now. I won't see her put out or gas & light shut off" (Wednesday 15, 1935 [no month noted] letter from Gwyn Clark to Langston Hughes, LHP).

———————

WESTERN UNION

MARCH 5, 1936

LANGSTON HUGHES = YMCA= 180 WEST 135 ST =

MOM ONLY HAS DOLLAR LEFT TO EAT SEND SOME MONEY
ANSWER BY WESTERN UNION[1]

MRS C CLARKE

[Note box on telegram]

$25.00 OR LESS

CAN BE SENT TO

CLEVELAND

FOR 94 CENTS

AND IT WILL BE THERE IN A FEW MINUTES

1. The same day Gwyn writes Langston that he is in Carrie's room and that "she is very sick has been heaving. She had Brown yesterday. Will be glad when you get here. She said please have the money here no later than this Monday. . . . I have to call up Dr. Brown for Mom. She said that she can hardly see or sleep. By the time you get this letter you will long have gotten the telegram. The reason for sending it is that Mom only had a $2 left. . . . Dr. Brown was here again today. . . . He said the cancer is not doing her any good, and that he thinks that she should go to the hospital where she can get the attention she needs. Answer right back and let me know at Auntimeals if I should let them take her" (March 5, 1936, letter from Gwyn Clark to Langston Hughes, LHP).

———————

[March 8, 1936]

Cleveland Ohio

Sunday

Oh! Baby, I am so sorry you are ill. I hope you are all o.k. by now. I was so afraid that you had an awful bad cold. But I have been quite ill, very ill, all due to your friend & fellow citizen Dr. Stanley Brown. First I must tell you that, on another piece of paper, while I finish this letter. Yes the play, "Little Ham" is in rehearsal for Mrs. Jelliff told me so herself, but last week she was severly ill, could not get out, so she said it hurt so bad because she could not go. Gwyn got so excited Thursday, he run out to telegraph you.

I was very ill, and instead said send mail. Now we are supposed to leave or move Tuesday. Ada expects to move tomorrow, if not I have to move as Jane Hunter has asked me out. Now Gwyn will have to go to Oberlin Monday, get the thing after work If he can get them brought. It will come at least $4.00. I'll have to pay Mrs. B—2 wks $4.50 unless she will take the coal in part payment

The rent will be here	$4.00
A pass	1.25
"" Gwyn	.50
A few eats	1.50
Radio	2.00
Gwyn's Trip to Oberlin	1.00

Poor Gusto is shot. I felt so bad about him. When you read this I hope you are well. I still suffer.

Yours
Mother[1]

The Story of One Stanley Brown

I called Dr. Brown, told him you suggested I ask him to call & see me and see how I was progressing. Well, he had a meeting here Wednesday here so he came up to see me. He asked very nice & friendly how "I felt &ct." Then asked if I had any pain I said "Oh! Yes." He said, "Oh! You should have something to ease them." I then told him if I took anything it would be against my Drs. As they said they did not want me to take sleeping thing unless it was impossible to do without, if so then to take Aspirin. He blustered around and left me about 10 pills—one ever 4 hrs, charged me $1.29 cents. Well, I went to bed and then woke up crazy with pain. I got one of Brown's pill got back in bed, went to sleep, woke up at 8 A.M. Started to get up, could scarcely see, the whole room was going around and I was nearly dead [and] just at that minute Kit called. I said "I'm dying I think" In two minutes the room crowded. Gwyn rushed out to call Dr. Brown to ask him what in the world did he give me. Well I was very sick until Thursday night at 7 o'clock. Begin to get better. After eight o'clock

Brown drifted in with the news he was sending me to City Hospital next morning. I said "you can't send me anywhere as you are not my Dr." He said "well I'll get a room and take you over there." I said I *won't* [double-underlined] go. Absolutely won't go. He went out the next morning about 7:30 the matron opened my door and said "I came up to help you dress for the Hospital." I said who said so she said Dr. Brown & Mrs. Hunter. I then said "I am not going but give me Dr. Brown on the wire." She did. I said "Dr. Brown are you going crazy or what." "Neither but you have to go to City Hospital at once as Mrs. Hunt won't let you stay here." I said "Well she has not been women enough to tell me that. But I'm not going under you no where. Dr. Freedman is my Dr. and if he sends my charts, my assignments I would go." Dr. Brown said "Oh!" He said for me to take you. Hadn't ever seen him. Then I went to Mrs. Hunter. She said she never told me to move that Dr. Brown told her I had an incurable disease and not let me stay here. (a dirty lying skunk). To try to hurt a lone woman like that. Just to get a patient. No other reason. And so, Dr. Freedman called me told me to be out to the hospital at 3. Was he mad. He called Mrs. Hunter and laid her out told her he had helped the Phyllis Wheatley, but if she would put one of his patients out on a lie like that and he says "No one knows her condition but me and she *is cured*." Poor me. I've sure had trials.

1. On March 13, 1936, Gwyn writes: "Dear Lang, Moma has been pretty sick. They are thinking about taking her to the hospital. They took x-rays of her chest. They think that she has pus on her lungs or some where near there. We will move with Ada Williams this week or the first of next week. I know I will. Mom may have to go to the hospital. She said send her money to pay Mrs. Ailey and to move her things down from Oberlin just as soon as you can."

On March 17, 1936, he writes: "Mother growing worse in great pain can't get hospitalization at Lakeside come home at once wire answer immediately by western union" (letter from Gwyn Clark to Langston Hughes, LHP). Langston's response: "Leaving morning wiring money send mama any hospital necessary regardless of cost. Langston."

[June 22, 1936]

Dear Langston: My Baby.

Just got your letter with the $17.00 check. I wrote you on Saturday. Gwyn has to have books for his classes. That is why I wrote. Specially. I go to Hospital every day. Will tell you about it when you come. I have been doing part of the work also. Feel fair. My Girl left on last Saturday. I have another little girl now that cleans. Do you know when your rent is due. I don't. One of your plays "The Soul gone home" will also be at the Karum soon it is already advertised. I thin[k] the 27 & 28. Not sure. Little Ham went off fine here very good & crowds I hear. There are two tickets here sent you by Hildelman. Victory Dinner Mothers Peace Day. June 25th. May go for you. Ha! Ha!

Also wedding invitation for June 30th. Fannie Lucile Wilkins & Mr. Hugh Booker. Be so glad to see you. Twill be lovely. XXXX Kisses. Love and all.

Kit pawned his new suit. I saw Louise yesterday for five minutes. Hope you come. Hope you sell Little Ham. Hope you finish your play.

Luck to you
Mamma

_____

[Postcard] Dec. 2, 1936

Dear Langston
Leaving [Chicago] Gene met me has been lovely. Hope you are all O.K. Love to all.

Me

_____

Cleveland Ohio
Saturday

Dear Boy—So relieved to get your special. Glad you are all O.K. Gee I had worried my self silly. Never mind the letter I said a lots of foolishness about your coming home if you were ill and needed my care. Of course you do not.

I am not doing any thing for Xmas don't expect to as I have no Xmas feeling at all. Gwyn has a nice little job and likes it. He has also been teaching archery at Mrs. Jelliff's play house. He picked up wonderfully this month in his studies. Much better grades.

I don't blame you. I know it is selfish to want you here Xmas you can be there with your friends and have a good time. It's dull here and you could come here any time you could. Hope you are well and have the Merriest Xmas possible.

I am not very well at all my self. Have not been very much since before Thanksgiving but just go on and try to get by. I do not want you to try to send us one thing for Xmas. I do not want any thing. Gwyn don't need a thing. He is fixed pretty well and warm. I am trying once more to start a bank account but its very slow. Could you send me two more books. If so O.K. if not all right. I have two sold for Xmas presents.

Hoping and praying for [us] all O.K.

I am yours lovingly
Mother.

Cleveland Ohio
April 20 [1937]

Dear Langston

My Dearest Boy:—How I miss you every day. Well Kit was here yesterday. Very subdued. Studied most of the time he was here. Val is to be married so he says and I guess he hates it quite bad. He got everything she had of his yesterday. Came home stayed in all the evening until they left at 11 P.M. Good for him eh? Elmer finished the pictures and is mailing them today. He is very indifferent about going to get his money therefore I think he has none. Nannie Burroughs[1] spoke here yesterday and was very good. Mason[2] came in yesterday morning.

Raynor & Elmer & I being here he started on you and commence criti-

cizing your writing. Of course we ate him up. "He said you were to con-
sistent in your writing." Only wrote what you saw or thought within you.
OH! We fixed him.

Kit says it costs $10.00 for him to graduate and he will have to have that
by May 1st or near that time. His Board is due April 30th. Has only six
weeks of school. Graduates June 6th A.M.[3]

Did you get the laundry in time? I sent it in all that rain Wed P.M. Then
Thursday they come dragging it back here that it was weighed wrong and
needed another stamp. I told them to take it to the P.O. & get my money.
Twas not my mistake. Then I gave them a stamp again in the rain it started
off. Its raining hard also today.

Saturday		
Grocery Bill		$7.02
Milk		.72
Paper		.18
Laundry		.98
Gwyn		.50
Eggs		.42
Ruby		.30

Thus went the $12.00. This week I shall shave off & off.

Now I want to get this mailed, the weather is terrible—rain—rain rain.
I have no umbrella yet. I will try to get one some time. Well, hope you got
on fine. I saw Mrs. Lomax and was glad to talk to her said Mell was getting
ready for you.

Now I must get this in the mail. Enclosed is clipping and will send more
mail if any important comes in. You got two letters. Did you not? The play
manuscript came back. Will you please write me if you can.

Yours lovingly

Mom—

1. Dr. Nannie Helen Burroughs (1879–1961) was a prominent educator, orator, religious
and political leader, and businesswoman. She founded the National Training School for
Women and Girls, Inc., in Washington, D.C., on October 18, 1909. Her motto: "We spe-
cialize in the wholly impossible." She was also the catalyst for the largest Black women's

organization in the United States—the Women's Convention Auxiliary of the National Baptist Convention.

2. The identity of Mason cannot be established. He is possibly one of Carrie's many cousins or perhaps just a family friend.

3. Gwyn did not graduate from Wilberforce, a university supported by the American Missionary Association and focused on providing a liberal education for Blacks. On September 15, 1937, he had been admitted to the Combined Normal and Industrial Department at Wilberforce University, free of tuition, as provided in Section 11 of "An Act to Aid in the Establishment and Maintenance of a Combined Normal and Industrial Department at Wilberforce University, Greene County, Ohio."

Cleveland Ohio

Sat 22 [1937]

My Dear Langston:—

I got your letter yesterday. Also got a nice letter from Kit. Glad you are enjoying your stay out there so well. We will be glad to see you home. Every one ask for you.

I read a poem at the Federation[1] last night, and every one like it. I called it "Society." I will be happy to let you see it.

Langston your last check you left me was for the 22nd. That's today. I have no more. About Wilberforce, if you cannot don't bother. For I know what it is to be without money. Sending 2 letters.

Yours

M—

Lost my Pocket book. Yesterday was 3 hrs getting it nearly. Had key, glasses, 1.00 in money and my check in it signed. Ha! Ha! I got it.

1. The Federation of Colored Women's Clubs.

Dear Langston: Just got your letter. So glad to hear from you.
All pretty fair here. Glad you seen the Mitchells wish I could see them. It would be lovely for Kit to go. Hope he can do so. They would help him so

much—every way, I think. Francis is much better and has her glasses and stepping out much. I will want to go June 3rd as the exercises are June 6th. I am very short of money as Elmer has not yet worked and we have had to eat. He is going to do the Air Port starting Monday he says.

Hope Uncle John comes to see me. I am getting this done so I can get it off very hurriedly. Your Mother's Day card came Monday. All day alone Mother's day.

Elmer spent Mother's day & 2 days with his mother in Columbus. Hope to hear from you soon.

Yours Mamma

Love to Mirtie

[May 25, 1937]

Dear Langston,

I have just received your letter and have tried to do what you asked. Hope it is all o.k. The rates of these things are so high some how. I am fair today. Have had back trouble for a few days. I think Gwyn is ready. He did not need shoes I don't know why. Kit wants to much and you alwys do it instead of saying "No" some time.

Is he going to Las Vages? What in the world became of Mr. John Hughes. He never came back here is he back home? It will be terrible long before you get home. Be time to leave again. Mason is here trying to get to N.Y. He is going to Chicago for Decoration Day. Do you come through Alburque if so bring Home with you. Ha! Ha! Elmer was here last night. Wanting to know what I had to eat, he will never grow up.

If I go, I will leave June 4th for Wilberforce as Kit's excersis will be the 5th. Will be there over that day. Got a lovely letter from McKeesport asking me over for the Decoration Holiday. There is an excursion from here— $2.50 round trip. Would love to go but no money to do so. I wish you were here then. Well, good luck to you and much, much, love. Write soon. I sent one of the pictures to the Dr. in Denver. By the way Clarence Langston's, who died on the paper Denver Statesman, has a widow & 2 children in Denver, her name is Nona, and she sings in the choir. You might see her.

I have been so lonely.

Write Yours,
Mom

Francis has been very ill. Julia is poorly to. Looks very bad. Ada, Effie &
all send love.

Monday night [1937]

Dearest: I was hoping against hope that you wouldn't go. Now since I got
your message, the bottom has dropped out of everything. I am truly sorry
you are to go in a way. I hope that it will turn out O.K.

Are you going to Paris? I hope so.

All fair here as yet Kit has got no work but he has run himself crazy. But
the Playhouse settlement had him sign up today for the Camp Counselor.
But it will begin July 17 to August 28th about $35.00 and room & board.
Best he can do so far. I sure feel sorry for this kid. He does want work so
bad. But it seems none of the boys can get work. The rain all the time keeps
the expo from doing any good so they can't employ no one there. Other
works seems no good at all.

All of us O.K. living cheap as we can. The apartments have not said a
word yet. Mr. Blunt has been sick and he just came out today. Promised
me screens. Opal was so sorry they did not see you. Her & Harold will be
up here tonight so they said. Junpta was here yesterday. Well Darling write.
I wish I could come to New York tonight.

Hope you have a very happy journey and I will be praying for you that all
will be well and you may come back all O.K. I will save and stint all I can.

Don't worry try to be free & happy.

Mrs. Lane says she sends her love to you.

Raynor is here this is all will look for letter. Julia is not well today.

Write & Love
I am now lonely
Mamma

I have no paper so I am writing you on anything I can find. Raynor is coming over and take me to mail these.

Francis says she will pay me something if possible the 3rd.

Louie I saw yesterday and he said no word about it and I won't bother him of course.

I have to see if I can collect from Elmer.

———————

Mailed the stories. Hope they were o.k.

Cleveland Ohio

Aug 21 [1937]

My Dear Son:

I am so worried. I have been ill for over a week. I can't bear for you to be over in that war zone.[1] I am so worried won't you leave there. Just think what it means to hear every day that Madrid is bomed and surrounded with troops &ct. We are all getting along fair I guess. Kit is still at Camp but will be back tomorrow. I am *at* Bessie's paying $20 per. When I pay next rent, (Sept) I'll have about $10.00. But Langston please [get] out of Madrid. Please do this for me. For I'm just worried sick.

Please write me from Paris.

Yours

Ma

Wrote to other address in Spain.

Selby Minor's wife died very suddenly yesterday. It's sad. I am sending you this letter for may be you want to ans. This took it out of the envelope so it won't cost so much.

1. Langston had been writing Carrie from Madrid. On August 14, 1937, he wrote asking her to let him know if she had moved, how Kit was making out at work, and how the money was holding out.

———————

Cleveland Ohio

I just come to mail the stories. I sent all from that right Hand drawer, except 2 I could find no duplicate to. Hope it will be o.k. for I am very poorly today with a heavy cold.

Yes, I got the $75.00. Thanks. Rent is $20.00 per. I was very far behind as your letter was one month and three days on the way. Will write more later. I am no good. Kit is well I guess. Still at camp.

Please write often if you can.

Yours lovingly

Mom

Bessie & Chas o.k. Elks[1] here now & Charley runs every night. I have an awful cold, run down from worry. Can collect no money from no one. Thousand thanks.

Yours

Mom

1. Carrie refers to a convention of the Fraternal Order of Elks.

Cleveland Ohio

Aug 22 [1937]

My Dear Boy:

Just got your letter dated July 24th and I was crazy I was so worried. I could not eat and I was sure you was prison barred in Spain. I was ill one week from worry. Don't ever do that again. I wrote Mr. Sullivan,[1] also your lawyer[2] to find you. Mr. Sullivan telegraphed me this A.M. that he had a card from you & you were O.K.

Langston don't go to foreign countries like things are now and not write. Please do [not] ever do that for I will be ill & worry will kill me if I have to worry over you.

Kit is fair. Still in camp. I am at Bessie's. I told you all about it in my letter twice before. I pay $20 per month & rent is due on the 17th.

But I was one month & one day getting your letter and I owed everyone. All set now. Thousand thanks. Elks are here. I have not seen any. Julia very ill.

Carolyn

Elks Parade is today and every one is up trying to go. It is a full house in Cleveland now.

1. Noel Sullivan was Langston's friend and ofttimes host.

2. Arthur Spingarn (1878–1971) provided legal counsel to Langston throughout his career and was a lifelong advocate for the rights of Black people. He served the NAACP as lawyer, vice president, and president. An avid collector, Spingarn eventually donated all his books and artwork and his art collection to Howard University. His brother Joel, a writer, and sister-in-law Amy, an artist and philanthropist, were also deeply committed to assisting Black Americans. Langston's education was financed by Amy in large part.

———————————

Cleveland Ohio

Sept 29th [1937]

Lots of mail here. Lots of dates for lectures. White wrote Mr. Jelliff to see would you keep that engagement.

Well Langston, I have been crazy. You not getting any letters through just got your letter today from Spain, and it was nine weeks since I heard from you. Even N.Y.—Liever,[1] Spingarn, Jelliffe have worried themselves and every one else. Cablegramed & all. Mullatto is running. Liever wants to get in touch with you. The bank has $185.00 in your saving account. There was a check sent to your commercial acct. and deposited.

Kit is here as he did not get to go to School.

I have been to the Hospital and had a minor surgical operation. Cut out an infection. Had quite a little time, three or four stitches was in bed, but am some better now. Around the house now.

I don't want to write much as I do not know why you do not get my letters. I have written & written to Spain, to France. Kit has written about a dozen times. Hope you get our letters in Spain. We are out to Charlie's. Please write or come home.

Yours lovingly

Ma

C M Clarke

1. Maxim Lieber was Langston's literary agent, described by Arnold Rampersad as "a taskmaster" (ARI 281). Lieber, however, worked tirelessly and effectively to place Langston's work.

———————————

Cleveland Ohio
Nov 3 [1937]

My Dear Boy—:

Just got your letter.[1] I am so glad to know you are all right and hope on safe ground. I have worried my self nearly to death and I do not think I have any mind at all now. I am just dafy. I saw Louise last Thursday night and she was very kind. Gave me some money. They took up $309.00 at the meeting. I went down merely to see her.

Kit is working has had a job regular for about three weeks.[2] He has not had a pay yet of course it is not much, but sure will beat a blank.

I have as you now know been cut on in a minor operation, therefore have been no good. But am getting better now I guess. Yes, I am now at Bessie's but don't know how long, as there is no heat but gas and do not know how it will be in cold weather unless they do something about it. It has been very cold here already. I am paying $20 for three rooms, *heat*, light & gas. Kit was very sad about not going to School. He is bound to go to the seminary, did well. Commence taking private lessons next week he says from some Bible School here. Everyone has been so anxious about you. And you have several letters about lecture dates here. So many have written me for your address from N.Y. &ct.

The play "Mullato" run so Mr. Spingarn told me for a few weeks also I saw it in the paper. Do not know whether it is still running now or not.

Well, I could not find no kind of pen so have to back this at the bank[3] let me know our plans please when you write again.

Last month, I put $27.50 to your account. When there was another check sent you, bringing your account up to $222.53 cents that was Sept 30th. Now I am going to the bank and get the last report. You will see how you stand.

Did the man get the manuscripts? Write soon as you get this please.

Thanks for the check for it is all O.K. I'll be glad when I know you are back in the States.

Frances very sick.

Julia has been very ill. Better

Yours lovingly
Mother

1. Langston wrote Carrie on November 12, 1937, complaining that he hadn't heard from her: "Dearest Mama, Haven't heard from you for the longest time!! Why don't you all write? And how are you?" (letter from Langston to Carrie written from Madrid, Spain, LHP). Carrie had written, but wartime mail delivery was problematic.

2. Kit wrote Langston on November 10, 1937, asking for money to attend a dance, do laundry, "etc. and for paying $2 for busting a fellow in the mouth with my fist (ofay)."

3. An expression that means she has to sign or endorse the back of the check.

Cleveland Ohio
10520 Englewood St
Jany 10th [1938]

My Dear Son:—

I am so glad to hear you will soon be in New York. No one can ever make you understand how I worried about you while you were in Spain. I did not know what day you would be struck with a bomb. Don't never do that again, and once two months and two went by and I never heard a word then I was sick. Then Xmas I had not heard from you for over a month. Each day I expected to see you. Then no letter came and Xmas morning came and we had not heard. Then I went to pieces, had hysterics. Poor little Kit he did not know what to do. Then about 1 P.M. your cable came. Then I got out of bed and tried to cook something. We had no Xmas at all, except we got quite a few cards. We did not do one thing. Worried about you. Kit worked all day Xmas & all night Xmas night. And most of the next day. He worked New Years & New Years night also next day after New Years. I got your letters also a note from the bank.

I went down and they transferred $183.87 on my book.

Now on your saving account I have deposited $50 from the Afro American, $27.50 twice from songs. And $5.00 from the "Soul gone Home" from Los Angeles. Then I have one more check here for $27.50 came and I did not deposit. There were some more deposited. I do not know for what or how much. And you have tons of mail. It would cost $50.00 to send to you.

Kit went to school. He save $37.00 and Pet gave him $10.00 and he got ready and went back to school.[1] He asked Rev. Walker to get him a job for board. He was bound to go. I was glad he wanted to go. He worked since

Sept 16th. He did not make much, but he worked very hard. Then after Xmas they wer going to lay him off, so he wanted to go to school. I was glad. So when I got the money from the Bank I gave him $25.00. so he has enough now almost for this quarter. I hope he gets a job. Kit is much changed, quieter & seems to want to do something. He got so he did not go out at all. He was to tired after work. I got your "Not Without Laughter" published in Chinese from Shanghi.

The Playhouse settlement wants a play from you soon as possible. Jimmy's mother died. Mrs. Reese.

The Plain Dealer is trying hard to get in touch with you and said it was important. I told them I'd let you know when you get to N.Y.

Mrs. Jelliff has been very ill for two months. She is just getting about and is better now.

Elmer had his name in the book, "Who's Who in Art" this year and Raynor says he was the only Negro that they could find. Elmer is still crazy and has never paid me at all. Sadie Whiteside had operation on her eye. She can see now. Her son Clarence had two operations on his throat and can talk now. I payed one month back rent. Paid up the grocery bill. Paid some on Insurance and have been waiting to hear from you before I used any more, as I thought you might need it to get home.

Mulatto run two or three months this summer and your lawyer, also Mr. Leiver[2] was much worried as there was no one collecting for you. Playhouse Gilpins played Stevedore and it was terrible. During the play Tiny's mother died. She had to come out. Paul Banks got drunk every night and some of the white People in it were awful. To bad you missed the Omega Si &ct all three fraternity meetings. It was swell. Rev. Osmond and Walker danced every dance and everyone tried to faint. St. James Church burned down. Now I have told you plenty. More than you can read & digest.

Write

Yours Always
Mother

1. In an obituary for Carrie about six months later, Gwyn was listed as still in school: "now a student at Wilberforce."

2. Here Carrie refers again to Maxim Lieber, Langston's literary agent.

———————

Cleveland Ohio

10520 Englewood

Feby 3, 1938

Dear Langston: Yes I remembered your birthday, but I was not well enough to get out for a card, so I just wish you all the happiness in the world.

I did not get the apartment. It was alright to me for I can stay here until Shiloh comes. The only reason I wanted to move was in case you came home we'd have room.

I don't trade out here no where. I still go to Frank's on 83rd if I buy much. Of course alone I eat very little, so don't need much.

Of course I will make the money go far as it will. It's not for me it's been or being used. I never have none for my self. It's for Bills. Bills. Rent &ct. It will last I think if not it will be o.k.

I never see any one. I go to Cedar Ave sometimes once a week when I am well. No one comes out here. So I scarcely ever see any one. Glad you are busy. Hope you get all you plan done. Is your elbow well yet? Bess & Charley are all right. They treat me O.K. and we have never been angry as I know of. If so I'd not found it out. They have a car but go out very seldom. I can never go out in the evening for I am afraid to come home. And the hour cars start at 12.30. I think I have attended one thing at night. "Scottsboro" meeting was 3 weeks ago. Then Art Taylor and wife brought me home and Eddie Mason took me to "Stevedore" at play house. So you see I get out very little and am nearly crazy being so lonely, sometimes. But I can't stand it. Car fare is so high one can't go often now days. St. James Church burned down. Gilpins are playing Fisher's[1] plays again. "Conjurer Man Dies." I have not seen any cousins for about three weeks. I heard Frances was better. Well, I guess have told you all the news. My arm is almost so I can't use it at all any more. Yours Truly-lovingly

Mother.

Sadie has pneumonia in Oberlin. Very ill. Don't worry at all about me. I am O.K. Hope to see you when you do get home. Love to Toy.

1. Rudolph Fisher (1897–1934) was, by avocation, a fiction writer, whose *The Conjure Man Dies* has been described as the first Black detective novel. A play based on this work was first produced in 1936, more than a year after his death. By vocation he was a roentgenologist—that is, a medical doctor who used the new X-ray technology for diagnostic and therapeutic purposes. Ironically, he specialized in a therapeutic practice that would later be used to treat Carrie's cancer. Fisher's death, probably from cancer too, occurred in the same week that Wallace Thurman died. Langston lost two friends in seven days.

[February 7, 1938]

Langston: I have a little block cut I should imagine, from the American Society of Composers, &ct. Has about 6 letters on same.[1]

Here is some mail.

Mother

1. A block cut is a type of artwork, as described in the November 11, 1935, letter.

Kit has cleaned up the apartment

April 7th [1938]

My Dear Langston:

I wonder why you did not write me a few words. Are you alright, I worried about you. I am some better. I can eat I tell you. Tell Bessie I am waiting to hear from her. I had to get Gwyn's things[1] and the thing he brought out and have them brought up to town which cost over $2.00. So you see that's where my money went. We had a big snow yesterday. There were dust storm, rains, snow, blizzards, extreme heat, in different part of the world all in one day.

Have seen Toy once. No one else but Helen. Write me when you will be home.

Please just a note

My love
Mamma

Friday morning I just got your letter and was so glad to hear from you for
I had worried about you. You are so tired and worn out that I fear you
can't hold up. You must rest some please. Your play opened this week in
Brooklyn. We cut out the advertising from several papers.

Dr. told me twice I can go home any time I wish.[2]

See Erma, Julia, Francis and bring my bible from Francis.

Your Chicago poster is swell

Lovingly
Mom

1. Wilberforce University wrote Carrie on April 8, 1938, that Gwyn had withdrawn from
school to return home: "He reported his reason for this procedure that you were ill and
needed his presence there."

2. Langston had received a letter from Dr. Charles Herbert Garvin, MD, on March 10,
1938:

> My dear Langston: I am very sorry that I must write you that your Mother is
> not doing so well. She is very painful in her chest, necessitating rather strong
> sedatives. She is able to be up and around but has paroxysm of severe pain.
> So far as the pain is concerned we can take care of that with medicine, but
> x-rays taken a few days ago by Dr. Friedman at Lakeside show several areas
> of metastasis to her lungs. This means that her carcinoma is beyond control
> and it is only a question of time before she will succumb to its ravages. When,
> I cannot predict. It may be months or even years, we hope, but I am of the
> opinion that she is incurable. As you can perhaps recall she was an inoperable
> case in the beginning and it is most gratifying that x-ray therapy has kept her
> fairly comfortable for these more than two (2) years. X-rays can do no more
> now, I am certain.
>
> She is able to travel and I am certain from what she has told me about
> your plans for her, she would be better off in New York. There is no one here
> to cook and look after her.
>
> I am sorry Langston that I cannot write you a more optimistic letter. I
> have said none of these things to her and I think it is wisest not to. . . . Don't
> forget us. You have my best wishes for continued good health and success. I
> am always glad to read about you and would be happy to hear from you.
>
> Very sincerely yours,
> Chas. H. Garvin

CODA

Carrie had gotten worse by the time Langston moved her into his newly leased Harlem apartment in March 1938. She collapsed for the last time on Friday, June 3, at around four in the morning. At age sixty-five, the cancer that had consumed her body took her life. She died at Deaconess Hospital in Manhattan, where Langston had rushed her a few hours earlier. Langston then did what a dutiful son is supposed to do: he took care of the business of burying his mother.

On Sunday, June 5, at 4:00 p.m., Rev. Peter Price of New Mother AME Zion Church officiated at Carrie's services. Mable Diggs Bergen, accompanied by Dr. Melville Charlton, sang Carrie's favorite songs: "Goin' Home," "City Called Heaven," and "Beautiful Isle of Somewhere." Carrie was buried in Brooklyn's Cypress Hill Cemetery, Lot No. 921, Section St. Phillips. Langston even paid six dollars for a biweekly cutting, cleaning, and trimming of the grave and installation of a new lawn on it. The cost of Carrie's funeral was $257.34, including casket, embalming, grave, hearse, and limousine (ARI 360–61).

Langston did not cry at Carrie's funeral, maybe because of the lessons of dispassionate restraint he had learned at his grandmother's knee. More likely, he was just tired of crying for the way Carrie had neglected him most of his life, drained him dry financially and emotionally, and never refilled his emotional well. However, he would always know that he was truly the only being that really belonged to Carrie. He was her Dear Boy. Instead of tears and other outward passionate displays, he did reveal himself and the feelings he had about the most influential woman in his life: he used his art to work out his complicated familial relationship.

EPILOGUE

If this book's prologue—a formulation of Carrie Hughes's manner of influence—can be said to issue a *call*, its epilogue becomes Langston's subtle, previously unexplored *response*—not through his correspondence but through the resonance of his art. Because his essential nature was to be emotionally unrevealing, Langston deliberately constructed a concerned but careful relationship with Carrie in his own correspondence.[1] His well-known penchant for not allowing even his closest friends and companions to penetrate his inner self extends to the woman who gave him birth. From this sense of self-protection emerges a truism: Langston's art, in the 1920s and 1930s, often functions as a vehicle for implicitly revealing his most intimate thoughts and emotions.

For most scholars, Langston's practice of concealing his inner self is not a novel idea. It has been a guide, for example, to those who claim him for their promotion of a gay politics and art. They see the very private sexual life he carefully guarded as harboring a secret homosexual identity. Generally the frame for these arguments consists of a number of poems that appear to have homoerotic themes; poems cited most often include "Poem (To F. S.)," "Desire," "Star Seeker," "Shadows," and "To Beauty." Even though each lacks the expressive pointedness of, say, Ma Rainey's song "Prove It on Me Blues" or the seductive lyricism of Richard Bruce Nugent's novel excerpt "Smoke, Lilies, and Jade," his poems sustain a number of astute critical and theoretical readings.[2]

Nevertheless, despite the creativity brought to their readings, most critics are disingenuous in their conclusions as they lift the veil Langston so carefully constructed. Having peeked behind it, they hypothesize a private life he never formally confessed.

Although self-protective, Langston emerges as a more reliable interpreter about writing himself into his art when he gives readers the comic innovation of Jesse B. Simple. He explains the colloquy of Simple and Simple's friend Ananias Boyd this way: "The character of My Simple-Minded Friend is really very simple. It is just myself talking to me. Or else me talking to myself. That has been going on for a number of years and, in my writing, has taken one form or another from poetry to prose, song lyrics to radio, newspaper columns to books" ("Simple and Me" 257–58). Arnold Rampersad offers this interpretation of Hughes's aesthetic revelation:

> For all the humor, Simple and his questioner form a sort of colloquium of Langston's surface conflicts of belief, as well as his deeper fears and desires. The uninspired narrator is Langston Hughes without love, laughter, and poetry—the man his father had wished him to be, the man he himself feared he easily could have become. Simple, on the other hand, personifies the genius of the black folk for self-redemption in the face of adversity, a genius that Langston, with the passion of an intellectual outsider, an *aficionado*, had devoted his life to honoring. (ARII 65)

This doppelganger structure enables Langston to present the lives, language, and lore of the low-down people he so revered and found necessary to his conception of art, while at the same time it sets forth the formality of his own bourgeois grounding. In effect, this writerly strategy is a form of masking. It is true of both voices that Langston veils or protects himself from the penetrating eyes of those who would seek to know him more intimately. His masking permits him to share as much as he cares to about his inner life.

In this spirit, an equally convincing narrative unfolds, in which Langston reveals a concealed emotional self in the aesthetic response he makes to Carrie's incessant plight, demands, and needs. As shown above, her letters inscribe an emotional web that entangles Hughes's life. "The odd thing is," according to Rowena Jelliffe, "Langston never complained" (qtd. in ARI:38). But why he did not *directly* answer his mother takes on new meaning when examined from a Bowen perspective. C. M. Gill explains: "Bowen points out that the parents' focus on an undifferentiated child often takes the form of an 'angry, conflictual struggle. As the parent over-focuses on the child, the child's functioning is stunted . . . crippling the child emotionally'" (92). Quite possibly this accounts for Langston's well-known predisposition to internalize his emotions. Nevertheless, while he did not reject or ignore Carrie, Langston did answer her *indirectly*. To manage her overbearing, self-centeredness, he resorted to art.

Not without Laughter

A typical analysis of Langston's first novel, *Not without Laughter*, might begin by referring to his essay "The Negro Artist and the Racial Mountain," where Langston carefully lays out a vernacular theory of art. He distinguishes middle- and upper-class Blacks from the "low-down folks" who embody for him racial authenticity and uniqueness. Bowen's theory, however, permits another strategy for interpreting the novel. It enables us to see how Hughes reinvents himself and his family for aesthetic and therapeutic purposes and thereby reveals something of the intimate life he cautiously preserves.

On the question of creating a reinvented self, Langston once again is his own best spokesman. In *The Big Sea*, he recalls that sometime around 1926–27: "I wanted to write about a typical Negro family in the Middle West, about people like those I had known in Kansas." In what proves to be a significant qualifying statement, he says: "But mine was not a *typical* Negro family" (303). The sage advice most first-time writers receive is "to write about what you know." Langston knew intuitively the core values he wanted to represent in his fiction, and he also knew that his own family's middle-class sensibility did not represent those beliefs. Carrie could hardly be said to embody warmth, maternal instincts, and unconditional love. Her father's death caused her to lose the life of relative privilege she had enjoyed as a youth, so she turned into a self-absorbed, demanding woman, who sought life's pleasures at the expense of others. Langston's father, filled with rage and even self-hatred and racial hatred, also did not illustrate the endearing qualities of a family head. His raison d'être was the acquisition of money and property. Material pursuit became his obsession, rather than making family the object of his affection. The one person who came closest to Langston's own values was his grandmother Mary, but even she was not "typical." She neither attended the more spirit-filled African American churches nor did she speak in Negro dialect or take in washing. Looking back to his childhood, Langston found isolation and a predisposition toward loneliness in the place normally occupied by joy, happiness, and unconditional love.

Langston confronts the fact that his extended family's prestige and prominence did not translate into strong, individuated lives. They could hardly be useful sources for representing the "typical" lives he needed for his novel. For narrative purposes, then, he reinvents his own family. Carl Van Vechten might have been helpful to the writing of *Not without Laughter*, when, encouraging Langston to write his autobiography, he gave him permission to expand the stories past his real-life experiences—to lie, in a sense. "Try to be as frank as possible," he wrote Hughes in a 1925 letter, "but when your material runs a little thin, don't be afraid to imagine better material or to put down someone else's experience as your own" (CVV 17). "Characters tend to resemble people in certain ways and the trick," Van Vechten told Langston a few weeks later, is "to make them enough different so that they won't be recognized" (CVV 21). Perhaps the line between "reinvent" and "lie" is simply a distinction without a difference, but it cannot be disputed that Hughes redefines his family for inclusion in *Not without Laughter*.

Take Carrie, for example. Unlike the alter ego of Jesse B. Simple, Carrie becomes the basis for three characters in *Not without Laughter*: Tempy, Annjee, and Harriett. The Carrie who participates in the literary society founded by her father, introduces her son to the love of libraries and librarians, and adopts the values of the Black upper middle class becomes Tempy in the novel. Tempy, the eldest child of Aunt Hagar, has risen in the social structure of Stanton, Kansas, by way of her acquisition of property and money. Her upward mobility has distanced her from the family that gave her a start in life. Tempy is the part of Carrie that is caught up in a bourgeois social station and, as Aunt Hagar says, "don't 'sociate no mo' with none but de high-toned colored folks." She was "that kind of a nigger—she's up in the world now!" and acted superior to Black folks, including her own mother, who "still earns ma livin' with ma arms in de tub."[3] Working as a maid for her aptly named White mistress, Mrs. Barr-Grant, Tempy finds all the motivation she needs for success in the words her employer shares with her several times: "You're so smart and such a good, clean, quick little worker, Tempy, that it's too bad you aren't white" (239). Blinded by her need for the approval of Whites, Tempy construes appreciation from these words and misses their irony. The narrator explains: "[She] had taken this to heart, not as an insult, but as a compliment" (237).

In the novel, then, Tempy *nearly* becomes the symbolic representation of the Black middle class that Langston uses for his "straw man" argument in "The Negro Artist and the Racial Mountain." Tempy's nephew Sandy is, for her, a "work-in-progress." Tempy's mission, as she understands it, is to instill in Sandy the virtues of modeling his life on the values of being White, of coming up to the level of White people: "dress like white people, talk like white people, think like white people—and then they would no longer be called 'niggers'" (240). This means divesting him of the spirituals and blues, teaching him "proper English," worshipping at the more "refined" Presbyterian church, recommending W. E. B. Du Bois as a political model instead of Booker T. Washington, and urging him to read English classics and modern novels. Although racial uplift and material pursuits consume Tempy's energy, Langston tempers her character a bit by showing through her stern demeanor a heartfelt emotion for Sandy and sincere desire for him to succeed in acquiring an education. Thus, in softening Tempy's character, Langston also transforms the image of Carrie.

Annjelica or "Annjee" becomes smitten with wanderlust as she, like Carrie, follows her man from town to town and essentially abandons her son to her mother's care. In life, Carrie causes Homer, her second husband, to lose his center, especially when she triangulates Langston into their relationship. Eventually, Homer abandons her. In the novel, as long as Annjee stays put, Jimboy has a center to his vagabond life and always returns to it. That she counters his wanderlust with stability, the narrator tells us, "was why Jimboy married her, because she wasn't a runabout. He'd had enough of those kind of women before he struck Stanton, he said. . . . She was the first nice girl he'd ever met who lived at home, so he took her" (33). Annjee's decision to pack up and follow him causes Jimboy to lose that place, that "home." He spends the rest of his life wandering, to be lost in the chaos and horror of World War I.

In an arguably satirical portrait, Annjee also becomes a re-creation of Carrie in terms of their shared ambition for stage performance. Langston positions Annjee as a member of the Royal African Knights and Ladies of King Solomon's Scepter, an organization whose high-flown names are a parodic representation of such established groups as the Masons, the Order of the Eastern Star, Charles Langston's Inter-State Literary Society, and others which lent dignity and respect to African Americans in a world that often demeaned them with various manifestations of Jim Crow. The participation of Annjee in "A Drill of All Nations," representing Sweden, is more than a bit ironic. While her life is mired in de jure and de facto racism, she represents a country that appears to be devoid of interracial conflict. More to the point, hers is a performance that seems modeled on Carrie's dramatic presentation of "The Mother of Gracchi," which Langston, as a child, disrupted. Because he didn't like the poem, which represents the speaker as a devoted and caring mother, he undermined the high seriousness of her theatrical moment by mugging to the audience in the middle of Carrie's recitation: "I began to roll my eyes from side to side, round and round in my head, as though in great distress. The audience tittered. My mother intensified her agony, I, my mock agony. Wilder and wilder I mugged, as the poem mounted, batted and rolled my eyes, until the entire assemblage burst into uncontrollable laughter" (*Big Sea* 25). Langston's "performance" earned him the worst whipping of his life, from which he learned a lesson in respecting other people's art and, more importantly, in hiding his true emotions in the process.

If Tempy and Annjee represent the bourgeois, theatrical, wandering parts of Carrie, then Harriett becomes the rebellious adolescent informed by Carrie's demanding, egocentric, good time–loving, irrepressible spirit. Harriett is clearly one of Langston's favorite characters because she, more than her fictional sisters, represents the text's fascinating portrait of blues life and culture. The chapter titled "Dance" contains his exposition of the blues as more than a representation of cultural expression; it becomes a philosophical construct. Harriett figures prominently in a discussion that is at once earthy, low-down, and existential. The narrator, sounding very much like Langston's voice, plumbs the depths of experience when he says: "The earth rolls relentlessly, and the sun blazes for ever on the earth, breeding, breeding. But why do you insist like the earth, music? . . . Who understands the sun? Do you, Harriett?" (90). In this blues interlude, Harriet personifies the meaning of existence itself. While Langston probably does not intend such high praise to mirror Carrie, he uses aspects of Harriett's rebelliousness to suggest Carrie. Harriett clearly opposes Aunt Hagar's rootedness in Christian forbearance and forgiveness. She, unlike her mother, simply cannot endure the many acts of racism confronting her and all Blacks. Harriett becomes the antithesis of the church-inspired version of respectability that her mother teaches when she enters a life of prostitution at age sixteen. She retreats to life in the Bottoms, where, paradoxically, folks "ceased to struggle against the boundaries between good and bad, or white and black, and surrendered amiably to immorality" (216).

Carrie, as adolescent, battled her own mother, especially after her father's death. Mary Langston had almost no appreciation for Carrie's values, goals, and ambitions. Carrie was fun loving and outgoing. She loved plays, musicals, parties, and novels. She longed for the professional stage, loved to be in front of an audience, and took her acting seriously. Langston's novel tells us that Harriett succeeded against overwhelming odds and earned the sobriquet "Princess of the Blues," suggesting that the pain and suffering she endured culminated in a thriving career in a significant art form. Carrie, by contrast, worked studiously for one shining moment: a part in Hall Johnson's folk musical *Run, Little Chillun*. En route to their respective achievements, we find that Carrie inappropriately fused with her family members, while Harriett's life at novel's end becomes the perfect embodiment of a strong, self-differentiated woman. For narrative purposes, her success is necessary to counter Annjee's wish for Sandy. Annjee reenacts Carrie's mantra to Langston: "get a job and help support me." Harriet's success makes possible Aunt Hagar's dream for Sandy to get an education and prepare for a life of service to the race. Unlike Sandy, Langston had no Harriett on his side, so he had to provide for his own education, formal and informal.

The novel's principal male characters, Jimboy and Mr. Siles, in their own way, become products of Langston's reimagining as well. The male corollary of Harriett, Jimboy is Hughes's archetypal "traveling man." Ostensibly, he is a character without roots, since he is liable to up and leave when he hears a train whistle. While he is in place, though, his guitar energizes the neighborhood with the latest blues, and, with Harriett as apt pupil, the newest dances too. When the blues claimed him, "the guitar in Jimboy's hands echoed that old pain with an even greater throb than the original ache itself possessed" (62). Hagar, his mother-in-law, is centered in a religious faith that runs afoul of his secular grounding, leaving her to feel that Jimboy has no moral center. Despite having no fully developed family cohesion, he emerges as fairly well differentiated. Jimboy teaches Sandy about honesty, when Sandy buys candy with the money he is supposed to put in a church offering. He gives the last of his meager wages to help pay for Sandy's schoolbooks. Thus the wanderlust that bespeaks a wastrel becomes much more complicated, and Jimboy emerges as more than an irresponsible husband and father. He shows himself to be a man in ways Langston's father never was.

Langston's stepfather Homer appears to be a real-life model for Jimboy in that he loved to have a good time, play music, and dance. Both men were victims of discriminatory labor practices and continually moved about searching for steady employment. Their constant moves affected their marital relationships in similar ways. In an attempt to build family cohesion, Carrie, like Annjee, left her son behind with her mother to follow her roving husband. Neither Carrie nor Annjee could keep up with her husband, and both men eventually disappeared. There were sporadic reports of Homer, an ironic name for a traveling man, who, at different times, was spotted in towns from Oberlin, Ohio, to El Paso, Texas. At one point, when no word about Homer was available, Carrie simply assumed that he was dead.[4] In the novel, Jimboy went to Europe to fight in World War I and was never heard from again. In real life Homer was lost to Carrie and Gwyn just as Jimboy was lost to Annjee and Sandy.

Langston's father, James Hughes, had none of the romantic attributes of Jimboy or Homer. A traveling man of sorts, James finally settled in Mexico in 1903, where his entrepreneurial life enabled him to avoid the omnipresent U.S. Jim Crow laws. James carried the five-year-old Langston to safety during the 1907 Mexican earthquake—and in the novel Jimboy carries Sandy, who had been injured stepping on a nail—but there otherwise appears to be no close physical or even emotional contact between these fathers and sons. James is more like Mr. Siles, Tempy's colorless, materialistic husband. Like James, Mr. Siles looks condescendingly at lessfortunate Black people and loves money and property. Neither seems temperamentally suited to establishing strong, well-differentiated families. For example, Mr. Siles is unable to provide a maturing Sandy with practical advice about life, love, and sex. With his wife Tempy, he relies instead on such conduct books as *The Doors of Life*, which offers the Christian life as the way to a healthy sense of morality and a guide to all questions about growing up: "'Avoid evil companions lest they be your undoing [see Psalms 119:115–20]; and beware of lewd women, for their footsteps lead down to hell [see Proverbs 7:25–27],' said the book" (258). James's solution for a developing Langston was to preach the efficacy of money and acquisitiveness and the supposed virtues of intraracial class superiority. As a result, these men represent the failure of their families to achieve a strong, proud selfidentification and an emotionally functional status. Sandy, like Langston, is left to acquire support and knowledge from other sources.

In re-creating Mary Langston as Aunt Hager, Langston found himself limited by family history and class. The grandmothers were different—even opposites—in skin color, speech, family history, ways of earning a living, and more. Nevertheless, Langston makes it clear that both women were well differentiated in their family systems. Both Aunt Hager and Mary had close friends with whom they shared their families. However,

Aunt Hager, while poor, had no need to triangulate her friends into her family system for survival, as Mary had done. Her friends were just that—a community of people she enjoyed, liked, and respected. After her husband's death, Mary triangulated her friends "Auntie" and "Uncle" Reed into her family system in order to survive the extreme poverty she and Langston experienced.

Mary cared for Langston as keenly as Aunt Hager cares for Sandy. Both women can be seen to function in the role of mother when left alone to nurture their grandsons. Aunt Hager, like Mary, dies before her grandson is grown, which forces him into the care of an aunt and uncle—"real" kin in the novel, functional kin in Langston's actual life. In reinventing his family life, then, Langston anticipates Bowen's theory about inappropriate family fusion: both he and his fictional alter ego fail to achieve strong self-differentiation.

Mulatto

The history of the writing of the play *Mulatto* is apocryphal, since there appears to be no clear record of its conception and creation. It seems to have emerged from Langston's poem "Cross" (1925) and possibly the short story "Father and Son." He eventually revised an early draft of "Cross: A Play of the Deep South," which he retitled *Mulatto* (1930). Thematically, the play certainly fits into the 1930s South, with its frequent practice of lynching and its irrational fear of miscegenation. *Mulatto* is, as Leslie Sanders writes, "a social drama, a harrowing, melodramatic story of patricide and suicide" (4), but what Sanders calls the play's "personal resonance", concerns us here. Arnold Rampersad helpfully describes this resonance as less a "mulatto's sense of racial ambivalence than his rage for full acceptance by his [White] father" (ARI 192). In identifying significant factors about the play, he names one that is especially poignant: "Hughes's ingrained sense of having been neglected by his mother and abandoned by his father allowed him to empathize with the tragic mulatto although he was not one" (ARI 192). At the heart of this play, then, are unresolved family conflicts.

In *Mulatto*, Langston works out some of his aggression and disappointment regarding both of his parents, his feelings of disconnection from them, and his assertion of individuation. The college-educated, articulate, biracial son in the play murders the father who refuses to acknowledge his paternity, and his mother goes mad. Bert, the son, returns from Atlanta (as well as from travels to Richmond and Washington) committed to the idea of not returning to the usual racial rules that would have him accepting a secondary place in his own father's house. His resistance to "knowing his place" in the South invites the retribution that culminates in his strangling his father and, in advance of a mob hell-bent on revenge, committing suicide in his mother's bed, in his father's house.

Once he figuratively kills off his own father in this play, Langston is able to desecrate the corpse by publicly announcing to the world that he hates his father. In these powerful pages, he resurrects the image of James Hughes as unfeeling, controlling, insensitive, materialistic, race hating, self-hating, and more—all of which makes Langston violently angry and equally sick. The play implies a bitter indictment of James; it accuses him of failing to facilitate either a healthy fusion of the family or Langston's development of strong individuation.

Even in his play, Langston found no relief from the tension in his relationship with Carrie. His inability to murder Cora, the mother in the play, resonates with his own inability to live his life without Carrie. So deeply does he love her and need her to love him back that he could not do without her in his life or murder her onstage. He could never give words the power of absolute destruction, to voice how he really felt about her—primarily because he did not want to feel that way. He did not want to think that he could ever hate his mother as he did his father. His need for love from her ran too deeply for that. Langston never understood the reality of their relationship, so he thought there had to be some type of madness controlling Carrie for her inability to love him as hard as he loved her.

With this play, Langston, whether he intended it or not, reveals characteristics of his own poorly differentiated life. His well-known gregariousness was rooted in his need for the affirmation of others. He must have thought, as most abandoned children do, that something was wrong with him that his own mother could not love him. Langston tried to be worthy of Carrie's love, but emotionally they were inappropriately fused and could never have an unconditional, reciprocal love. Their family system did not allow them to be individuated. Accompanying Langston's lack of self-individuation were feelings of guilt for not possessing unconditional love for Carrie. In "Cross," there is an expression of a son's regret at having ever disrespected his mother:

> If I ever cursed my black old mother
> And wished she were in hell,
> I'm sorry for that evil wish
> And now I wish her well.

Carrie seldom provided peace in her home for Langston. At worst, she denied him her love and much-needed emotional connection. At best, when Langston returned to visit, she gave him the bed she and Homer shared. Ironically, in the play, the best "protection" Cora provided was to give Bert her room and her bed in which to kill himself so that he could escape the horrors of the lynch mob and die in peace.

"The Negro Mother"

Arguably, no poem depicts the meaning of true motherhood for Langston more than "The Negro Mother" (1931), written when Langston's perpetual conflict with Carrie was continuing to prevent his development of an appropriately fused, strongly individuated self or to perceive one in her. Beginning in 1927, he had sought comfort and support in the irascible dominance of Charlotte Osgood Mason, whom he and others, at her insistence, called "Godmother." The strength of her personality overwhelmed his fragile self. With money and uncanny emotional control, she forced him into a subordinate relationship and effectively became his surrogate mother. Their imperfect fusion proved to be as inappropriate as the one he had with Carrie. In May 1930, when their relationship began to unravel, a clueless Langston cast about, seeking ways to explain and repair the mysterious damage to their relationship. He had placed so much trust in Godmother that the sudden rift between them caused the earth to feel unstable beneath his feet, and he became violently ill. "Shattered by her words," Rampersad wrote, "his body [betrayed] a neurotic turmoil that made his muscles twitch involuntarily and his fingers curl into bizarre shapes" (ARI 185). The one woman with whom he had exchanged pledges of unconditional love withdrew her affection and stipends, leaving a bigger void in his life than he had ever felt with Carrie.

Into this emptiness came Mary McLeod Bethune, with whom he developed an emotional connection representing his vision of a real mother.[5] Unlike the very needy Carrie and the overbearing Mrs. Mason, the model of Mrs. Bethune is that of a rescuer. Indeed, Rampersad claims that through "The Negro Mother," Langston "sought to banish Godmother and restore the black mother to her rightful place" (ARI 222). He chose Mrs. Bethune because she, not Carrie, rescued him in his time of need, nurtured his talents, and supported his desire to make his living through art. As an homage to her freely given support and to anchor himself in his ethnic heritage, he honored her generosity by locating the poem within the traditional role Black mothers have played in racial and family development. The poem distills the expressive history of their suffering and sacrifice, of their three-hundred-year journey from Africa carrying "the seed of the Free":

> Children, I come back today
> To tell you a story of the long dark way
> That I had to climb, that I had to know
> In order that the race might live and grow.
> Look at my face—dark as the night—
> Yet shining like the sun with love's true light.
> I am the child they stole from the sand
> Three hundred years ago in Africa's land.
> I am the black girl who crossed the dark sea
> Carrying in my body the seed of the Free.

For Langston, Mrs. Bethune symbolized not just personal or individual strength but strength of commitment to the larger racial family, the people who had not abandoned or used him. In her founding of the educational institution that would later bear her name, now Bethune-Cookman University, Langston identified an act of great vision, containing the potential for the uplift and success of all Black people. Her unceasing labor to build a pathway for African American advance enabled him to see in her the requisite qualities of true racial leadership. The mother's journey—a trek across age, time, and space so that her children are free and able to live and grow—has none of the inappropriate fusion that defines Langston's relationship with Carrie. The Negro mother does not complain about her sacrificial journey but offers her story as a means to explain their lives and the freedom—the full *differentiation*—they have. Mrs. Bethune understood and deeply appreciated Langston's generous praise. When Langston read "The Negro Mother" in Florida, with Mrs. Bethune in the audience, she responded by leaping to her feet and, with tears staining her eyes, declared: "My son, my son" (ARI 229).

In effect, Mrs. Bethune's response testifies to Langston's perception of what a strong, lifelong, individuated relationship might be like, but life and its attendant responsibilities intruded upon this idyll. He disconnected from the strangely fused, dysfunctional relationship with Charlotte Osgood Mason as his surrogate mother. After this abrupt separation, he retreated, ironically, to the care of the woman he initially sought to replace, the woman who had withheld from him physical and emotional sustenance—his real mother, Carrie. The peace and solace Carrie brought him were short lived; the relationship quickly became strained. Langston's angst at unsuccessfully building a cohesive relationship with Carrie is captured not only in his published poems of motherhood but also quite tellingly in an unpublished verse titled "Poem":

> I am waiting for my mother.
> She is Death.
>> Say it very softly.
>> Say it very slowly
>> If you choose,
> I am waiting for my mother,
>> Death.[6]

These few lines illustrate more than what Rampersad calls Langston's lifelong preoccupation with "melancholy, loneliness, and suicide" (ARI 14).

The spirit of resignation effectively pronounces a valedictory on the relationship Langston has with Carrie. Its finality signifies how he is consigned to a life of inappropriate fusion with her and how he will wait patiently for the end of their relationship—death.

Soul Gone Home

As much as Langston tries to represent his mother as generous, caring, and sweet, he could scarcely mask the feeling, as he said in his second memoir, *I Wonder as I Wander*, that she "seemed to have the fixed idea that a son is born for the sole purpose of taking care of his parents as soon as possible" (308). Finding new and seemingly prolific ways to spend his money, when he had it, Carrie nearly forced Langston into capitulating to her demands that he find a job paying a regular wage or salary, something guaranteeing a regular income. What kind of job, he asked, could he "find in the middle of the depression which would pay enough for three of us to live on—herself, my brother and me"? (307) The escalated pressure and frustration to triangulate Langston into providing for Carrie and Kit's survival pushed him to a resolution: "If in 1936 I do not make my board and keep, I shall withdraw from the business of authoring and try to take up something less reducing to the body and racking to the soul. I'll just let ART be a sideline, like it used to be in the days when I was a bus boy and was at least sure of my meals" (qtd. in ARI 319). "Authoring" versus "working" poses a dilemma that Langston resolved by choosing between his parents. He still proclaimed more affection for Carrie since, unlike his father, she "had a well-meaning heart, and was generous to a fault" (WW 308). The decision to continue writing, which he formally renders in *I Wonder as I Wander*, did not readily betray the depths of his internal struggle, his ambivalence. As was his wont, Langston's life histories are seldom revealing. Given its development of a mother-son conflict, the one-act play *Soul Gone Home* functions as a viable conduit into the intimate self he so carefully guarded. It is a serendipitous response to Carrie's efforts to triangulate him into meeting her demands.

After receiving word of Carrie's cancer, Langston refused to desert her. Instead he felt compelled to offer assistance during this crucial period. The

misperception that he had unlimited financial resources, though, continued to grate, forcing him, as Rampersad writes, to vent "his anger in a
macabre little play, 'Soul Gone Home,' in which a dead son sits up at his
wake to confront his mother, evidently a cheap whore, with charges of
hypocrisy and negligence" (ARII 319). In choosing the narrative strategy of
the dead talking back to the living, Langston perhaps deliberately elected
to write out of a time-honored literary tradition, one that goes as far back
as the biblical story of the rich man and Lazarus (Luke 16:19–31).

In this well-known narrative, the rich man goes to hell after his death
and finally sees the errors of his profligate life and his disregard for the poor.
Fully aware that his brothers follow in his wake, the rich man begs that
word be sent to them to repent and thus avoid the fate that has befallen
him. No doubt Langston had also read Edgar Lee Masters's *The Spoon River
Anthology* (1915), the book that had revived this narrative strategy via experi-
mental epitaph poems. In choosing to have his speakers offer warnings and
advice to the living, Masters also revealed something of himself. As John E.
Hallwas writes, *The Spoon River Anthology* is "a depiction of the struggle for
self-realization in a society that has lost contact with the great democratic
vision that once gave purpose and meaning to American lives, *and an account of the poet's quest to resolve his inner conflicts* and to restore that vision"
(2, emphasis added). Hughes was less interested in using *Soul Gone Home* to
comment on democratic vistas, although it was written during a heyday for
sociopolitical, agitprop, melodramatic, and overly moralistic problem plays.
It certainly fits into the dramatic kind in which the playwright explores his
own internal conflicts and issues through his art.

In effect, Langston uses this strategy to represent his pent-up emotions,
but he seeks to have it both ways. The protective shield he erects around his
feelings mitigates the resentment he has for Carrie's fusion of him into her
needs. For instance, eighteen or so years after he wrote *Soul Gone Home*,
he corresponded with Ulysses Kay about a possible operatic version of the
play. His description of the play cast an image that conflicted with what
appears to be the initial motivation of the play:

> [I]t is NOT a heavy tragic sentimental play. It is a TRAGI-COMEDY,
> with the accent on the comic elements in the boy's role, who is haunt-

ing his mother as much for fun as for spite. The SON is a slyly humorous, evil, badly raised little teen-ager who, if he had lived, would have been a street-corner jitterbug, a be-bop boy, a mambo dancer, a pool room sharpie—but who blames his mother, more or less justly, for his defects. . . . There should be as many laughs as possible in the way the SON's part is written and played—otherwise the tragic-comedy will not come through, and it will be merely an over sentimental and unpleasantly grim piece. ("To Ulysses Kay" 266)

The tragicomic focus Langston proposed was at great odds with the original play. The new intention effectively softened the textual critique of the mother in the earlier version, thus making the new one an evasive gesture. It moderated the extent to which Langston presented his resentment of Carrie's incessant demands and his own acquiescence to her needs. More simply put, the *letter* is self-protection, at best, in that Hughes was striving to distance his own emotional response from his real mother who mistreated him in the same way as the mother dramatically represented in the earlier version of the play.

Langston takes pains to characterize the boy negatively. Blues and later jazz, especially bebop, shape and inform much of his creativity. However, the very music that sustains his art functions here to denigrate the boy's image. Little good emerges from the description of him as "a street-corner jitterbug, a be-bop boy, a mambo dancer." Instead, it raises the question of why Langston overreaches in this effort to condemn the boy, not the boy's mother. Further describing the boy as "slyly humorous, evil, badly raised," as one who haunts his mother "as much for fun as for spite," shifts the burden away from the mother and places it squarely on her son. The gesture redeems the mother and blames her son. By seeking to ensure that the newer version emphasizes the comedic, Langston considerably lessens the mother's culpability in her son's death. The consensus among the handful of critics who have commented on the play confirms that, despite his intentions, *Soul Gone Home* is not tragicomedy.

Rampersad, as mentioned, sees the play as "macabre," a demonstration of the very grimness Hughes sought to escape. It is difficult to disagree with this characterization because the play's very setting bespeaks a haunting, Edgar Allan Poe–esque environment (without the horror): a tenement room, bare, ugly, dirty; an unshaded light bulb; and even the mother described as "loudly simulating grief" (*Five Plays* 39). Webster Smalley conceives the play as a fantasy. He maintains that it is not without some "ironical comic moments, but its impulse is far removed from comedy" (ix). The focus Smalley implies rests on supernatural phenomena, such as the setting or the plot. He adds to this: "Although a fantasy in concept and structure, its atmosphere and effects are those of naturalism" (ix). Naturalism becomes Smalley's way of introducing race into his analysis. Two peripheral White characters are probably not worthy of the weight he places on them, since their only role is to retrieve the dead son's body. Smalley makes them into symbols of a repressive environment, in effect changing the focus of the play from a mother-son familial conflict to a relationship shaped by the effects of racism.

Reading *Soul Gone Home* through the lens of Bowen theory provides another way of considering how Langston represents his own life through his art. Conceptually, the play lends itself to Bowen's idea of inappropriate fusion. As we state in our prologue, *fusion*, when achieved improperly, causes two people to lose their individual identities and purpose because one is assigned an unfair burden in caring for the other. There is no real balance in the relationship. Demands made on one to solve the problems of the other culminate in a sense of disconnection and an inability to retain one's individuality.

In *Soul Gone Home*, the two principal characters find themselves locked in a debate about the relative merits of their shared mother-son relationship. Ronnie, the dead son, establishes the play's conflict when he rises from his deathbed and declares to his mother: "I'm dead now—and I can say what I want to say." This assertion initiates their contentious conversation. In condemning her for being a poor mother, his list of accusations is quite extensive: "you ain't done me right"; "you been a bad mother"; "you never did feed me good"; "I had TB 'cause I didn't have enough to eat never when I were a child." He grew up bowlegged and stunted from "undernourishment," to which she replies: "Under-nurse-mint?" Arguably, Hughes intends this exchange to be a bit of the humor he later explains as crucial to the success of the play. Indeed, this malapropism is a comedic strategy he would exploit to great use in the Simple stories, where Jesse B. Simple is clearly joyously playing with language. As used here, though, the difference in language effectively demonstrates how different the son is from his mother. When he says her neglect leads to his growing up with neither "manners nor morals," she replies: "Ronnie, where'd you learn all them big words?" Carrie, as a college-educated, one-time teacher, certainly had better command of language. Hughes, of course, makes "[neither] manners nor morals" function to reveal his own critique of Carrie's negligence, irresponsibility, and exploitation.

Carrie's negligence is occasioned by her sporadic presence in Langston's life. Her pattern of appearing and disappearing creates an unstable existence and forces him largely to fend for himself. At precisely the moment he feels he is about to enter the world of education and therefore possibility, Carrie parallels the words of the mother in the play, who exclaims, "I kept you with me—off and on. . . . Now, just when you get big enough to work and do me some good, you have to go and die" (*Five Plays* 41).

Langston, of course, is not dead to Carrie. However, Carrie's inability or refusal to nurture and provide for her son renders his ambitions dead to her. Similarly, her motherly support and encouragement are dead, in a sense, to him. She is not performing as the mother in a well-functioning family system should. Instead, she creates the enmeshed relationship into which she pulls him. Their relationship becomes inappropriately fused, with Langston forced to take the lead in caring for both of them. His becomes a constant evasive dance, trying desperately to fend off her demands to give up writing and earn a steady income against his needs to remain an artist and thus attempt to retain his individuation. The play illuminates their fusion in an eerie confrontation. The motif of the dead son talking back to the living mother also gives Langston a measure of freedom and courage to unload his frustrations and articulate his disappointments. The last comment in the play arguably characterizes the mother as self-serving and smugly moralistic, but it also criticizes Carrie for her selfish, hypocritical attitude toward Langston: "Tomorrow, Ronnie, I'll buy you some flowers—if I can pick up a dollar tonight. You was a hell of a no-good son, I swear!" (42).

Webster Smalley has argued that the atmosphere and effects of the play are naturalistic. Instead of initiating a conversation about race, naturalism more plausibly reveals the nonfunctioning interdependence that defines this family. Just as Langston reinvented his family for narrative purpose in *Not without Laughter*, he reinterprets Carrie and himself as they engage in this macabre pas de deux. It was no coincidence that the play was written shortly before Carrie's death; it is an intentional working out of his frustrations with her.[7]

The decision to make the mother a prostitute "loudly simulating grief" creates a hollow but damning image. While she sells her body in order to make money for their support, she seemingly sells her soul too. After all, she has apparently made no other effort to earn a steady income to feed her son. Langston transfigures himself into a sickly, weak, malnourished, bowlegged boy whose premature death he blames on his mother. While the character Ronnie is starved for the sustenance that milk and eggs could provide, the playwright is starved on two levels: he laments the times he lived alone, knowing how to cook only "rice and hot dogs," and the times he went hungry in order to send money to Carrie (*Big Sea* 33). He is also starved for his mother's love and the stability of home. Ronnie and his mother, like Langston and Carrie, are inextricably linked in an interdependent relationship, but their inappropriate fusion prohibits a meaningful, satisfying familial union. Hughes appropriately titles the play *Soul Gone Home* because neither he nor Ronnie is fulfilled in their earthly lives. Only death will give them peace.

Not long before he died, Langston wrote a sharp, terse view of parenting that leaves no doubt about his feelings for Carrie and, to some extent, his father too: "My theory is that children should be born without parents—if born they must be" (ARI 4). This not-so-subtle indictment typifies Langston's mode of expressing displeasure with his family. It implicitly condemns them for not providing a significant, sustained system within which he could successfully function. His family system for most of his life included neither his mother nor his father. He spent part of his time with Arna Bontemps, Carl Van Vechten, and many other functional kin, but he also spent a very large part of his time alone. As an adult, whether he lived with or away from Carrie, he was constantly oppressed by her overwhelming demands. He, therefore, could not have developed as well differentiated. The lack of a strong family system for him was due largely to the choices that Carrie made.

Seemingly, their many differences and contentious debates reveal virtually no similarities in their lives. It is therefore the height of irony that they nearly shared one point of commonality: Carrie and Langston were allotted almost the same number of days for their lives. From Carrie's birth on February 22, 1873, until her death on June 3, 1938, she lived 23,842 days. From Langston's birth on February 1, 1902, until his death on May 22, 1967, he lived 23,852 days. His life was exactly ten days longer than hers (www.timeanddate.com). This longevity resonates with the whimsy of fate. These two people spent the entire span of their lives attempting to find common ground on which to stand and to build a close, familial, fully differentiated relationship. However, neither one was successful. It was as if their life paths suffered from parallel developments that were destined never to intersect and connect into a cohesive, loving family.

Moreover, their lives, as viewed through Carrie's letters, developed inversely in relationship to each other. Carrie's young days as a rather well-to-do "Belle" growing up in Black Lawrence, Kansas, set the tone she strove to fulfill but far too briefly experienced as an adult. When cancer claimed Carrie's life—a life wracked by pain and poverty—Langston, Kit, family, and friends paid tribute to her. Their "celebration," though, was more an obligatory or perfunctory gesture in which they obeyed the unspoken reverential rule of the Black community: "Speak no ill of the dead."

In contrast, Langston began his life much as Carrie's had ended. He grew up in the same town as she, but under very different circumstances. His early days were filled with misery, poverty, and loneliness. The functional families he created as a man did not fill the void he felt for not having his mother around, but they did provide a measure of the companionship and friendship he sorely needed. Unlike Carrie, Langston was adored by the world. He traveled across continents, met people who remained his lifelong friends, and produced work that was acknowledged and respected. When he died, ironically from cancer too, his life was genuinely celebrated by those people who praised his talent, respected him as a person, and supported his choices. Quite possibly those additional ten days permitted reflection, stock taking, and closure. Perhaps they enabled him to reach some accommodation with his difficult, failed struggle to have his mother make him feel that deep in her heart he was her dear boy.

NOTES

1. See especially the correspondence collected and published in Emily Bernard's *Remember Me to Harlem* and Charles H. Nichols's *Arna Bontemps–Langston Hughes Letters*.

2. It is virtually impossible to assemble a comprehensive listing of writers and texts here; however, a fair treatment of this issue can be found in John Edgar Tidwell and Cheryl R. Ragar's *Montage of a Dream: The Art and Life of Langston Hughes* (Columbia: University of Missouri Press, 2007).

3. Hughes, *Not without Laughter*, 37.

4. So much does Carrie believe that Homer is dead that she contacts Metropolitan Life Insurance, his insurance carrier, to check on possible benefit payouts. They reply: "[W]e have been successful in locating two numbers, one issued on May 20, 1907 and lapsed on May 24, 1909 and the other issued on October 6, 1894 and lapsed May 22, 1934. To date neither one of these policies has been submitted for its cash value. . . . The above is all the information that we are able to give you concerning your husband at this time."

5. Hughes met Mrs. Bethune in July 1930, when he and Zell Ingram were returning from their Caribbean trip. He was awestruck with her wit and "the wisdom of a jet-black woman who had risen from a barefooted field hand in a cotton patch to be head of one of the leading junior colleges in America and a leader of her people" (*WW* 40).

6. In a letter from Langston Hughes to Countee Cullen, February 12, 1923, "Correspondence–Publications–St. Louis Woman," Box 3, folder 4 in Amistad Research Center.

7. Carrie was spared this unflattering representation and, from what we can determine, never read the play.

SECOND CODA

In his first memoir, *The Big Sea* (1940), Langston frames the period of the Harlem Renaissance in terms of its effervescence as a cultural moment. "But certainly," he writes, "it was the musical revue, *Shuffle Along* (1921), that gave a scintillating send-off to that Negro vogue in Manhattan, which reached its peak just before the crash of 1929, the crash that sent Negroes, white folks, and *all rolling down the hill toward the Works Progress Administration*" (223, emphasis added). The image of the joie de vivre of the Harlem Renaissance being disrupted by the nation's precipitous fall into severe economic depression provides a descriptive frame for the fate Carrie suffers too. Even though she has a momentary flirtation with Broadway, she is actually more aligned with the economically disenfranchised: "The ordinary Negroes hadn't heard of the Negro Renaissance. And if they had, it hadn't raised their wages any" (228). Carrie's tortured life signifies what most historians commonly acknowledge: that the Depression started sooner among Black folk and affected them disproportionately. For instance, David M. Kennedy, in his well-respected *Freedom from Fear* (1999), posits: "Black workers, traditionally the last hired and first fired, suffered especially. . . . [Unemployment] fell with compound force on blacks, immigrants, and Mexican-Americans" (87, 164). In a poignant distillation of this thesis, historian Clarence Lang succinctly states: "Disaster hit African Americans earliest and hardest" (23). In a rather acerbic letter, Carrie speaks the dissatisfaction of many when she observes of the National Recovery Administration (NRA) that its indifference, if not its outright racial hostility, has earned it the epithet in the Black community of "Negro Run Around." Such socioeconomic forces contribute to the shaping influences on Carrie's life and the choices she makes. However, other determining factors help make up the complexity we attribute to her.

The abundant attention lavished on the teenaged "Belle of Black Lawrence" clearly imbues her with an expectation that she spends the rest of her life attempting to live out. Her father's death in November 1892 interrupts what now seems to be her self-perceived sense of entitlement. His unfortunate demise eventually forces her from a life of relative privilege into one of unrelieved poverty. She spends most of her adult years searching for an emotional or physical place that re-creates the earlier time when she stood onstage and basked in the glow of being at the social center of Lawrence. Instead of being the focus of admiration, she deteriorates into the rambling, ever-searching, always-importuning Carrie that emerges in her letters. As her years become filled with poverty, misery, loneliness, and bad health, she becomes even more entrapped by a poorly differentiated self, inappropriate fusion, and unfortunate efforts to triangulate her familial relations. Under these conditions, Carrie probably did the best she could possibly do to attain self-fulfillment. She had very little to work with: at best, an intense love of art offset by marginal talent and a misguided maternal instinct. While her actions may not necessarily evoke sympathy or even empathy, her letters provide a better understanding of who she was, her familial relations, her motivations, and, most important, a source for some of Langston's most inspired art.

ACKNOWLEDGMENTS

We have many people to whom we wish to express our deepest gratitude for their generous support and unfailing assistance as we worked to create this book. We wish to thank Timothy Young, curator of Modern Books and Manuscripts at the Beinecke Library at Yale University, for providing us insight into the difficulties of determining precise dates for the donation, processing, and availability of Carrie's letters. This book, like most contemporary Langston Hughes scholarship, builds on the work of Arnold Rampersad. At the University of Kansas, James Carothers eschewed the far easier "atta-boy" comments for a more thoroughgoing, careful scrutiny of the manuscript when we approached him for criticism. His readings of the book-in-progress were always thoughtful, cogent, and compelling, for which we can't say enough how appreciative we are. Susan Kumin Harris enabled us to discover more fully the complexity of correspondence as a genre, when she provided a model of her own scholarship on this subject. In the latter stages of book preparation, Clarence Lang offered some very pithy comments on the sociohistorical era from 1926 to 1938. His insightful observations greatly enriched our understanding of the period in which Carrie and Langston lived and wrote. For her thoughtful introduction to the literary critical possibilities of Bowen Family Systems Theory, we are grateful to Cheryl Lester for providing us a heuristic for probing beneath apparent simplicity to discover a more complicated vision of family life. Our debt to Pam LeRow and Paula Courtney of Digital Media Services is simply incalculable. Their preparation of the manuscript in its various stages was always done quickly, efficiently, and expertly. They were absolutely indispensable as they made our job so much easier. Of course, our colleagues in KU's English Department were wonderfully supportive, including the award of funds for a book subvention. When research questions arose, we depended, as always, on the historical acumen of Deborah Dandridge of KU's Kenneth Spencer Research Library. And in the eleventh hour, colleagues Nicole Hodges Persley and George E. Gibbs responded to our desperate plea for information on the history of Black theater.

My Dear Boy received its first full consideration at the University of Missouri Press, where two external reviewers subjected the manuscript to a rigorous analysis and concluded that it merited publication. The temporary closure of the University of Missouri Press led us fortuitously to the University of Georgia Press and the editorial expertise of Nancy Grayson. We are especially grateful that she saw the viability of this project and decided to bring it before an appreciative group of scholars, students, and nonacademic readers as a published book. Although retirement cut short her involvement in the process, she left *My Dear Boy* in the exceedingly capable hands of Sydney DuPre, Jon Davies, and freelance copy editor Chris Dodge. By now, we hope it is abundantly clear that seldom does a project of this kind come into existence without the cheerful assistance of a great many people, institutions, and resources.

I, Carmaletta M. Williams, wish to express my gratitude to those who inspired and helped me personally with the project. Exploring other people's family systems always demands that one's own family be examined. During the course of this project, I came to realize how deep were the debts that I owed to those women now passed on to Glory who considered me their "dear girl." My grandmother Blanche Pinkie Waters Blue stood as a wonderful role model of a fully, self-differentiated woman. My mother, Doris Rebecca Grant, learned those lessons and refused to develop improper triangulation and enmeshment, as she raised five children alone on a nurse's salary. My Mama II, the late Aileen Walker, had no children of her own but displayed a deep compassion for the children of her heart. My aunts, Jeanette Smith, Jerry Dianne Smith, Marion Jo Waters, and Vickie

Jones, appropriately functioned in their family roles. Vickie, Dianne, and my cousin Dorothy Frazier are the sisters of my heart. My own sister, Mitchi Payne, and her daughter Morgan, as well as my granddaughter-daughter Antoinette Jacine, center my life. I love them all dearly.

Of course there are men in my family who deserve a strong acknowledgment, especially my sons Dwight, Jason, and Nicholas. Their journeys to growing into fairly well differentiated men continue.

I am deeply grateful to Dr. Regennia Williams for introducing me to Carrie's letters. The amazingly positive response to our coauthored essay, "Mother to Son," in *Montage of a Dream: The Life and Art of Langston Hughes*, was the catalyst for *My Dear Boy*. I also send a note of deep gratitude to Dr. Joycelyn Moody. In addition to her friendship, I appreciate the caution in her book, *Sentimental Confessions: Spiritual Narratives of Nineteenth-Century African American Women*, which offers that the pull of sentimentalism is to convince the reader that the character has the "capacity to form a deep emotional, ethical or psychological alliance with another person or ideal" (10). I want the readers of this book to question that about Carrie by letting her tell her own story. I thank my friend and colleague Dr. Robert Xidis for patiently listening, discussing, and directing me to search for answers. I owe a deep debt to his wife, Dr. Kathleen Xidis, who shared her research and writings on the political history of the FDR administration.

The opportunity to research this project came from wonderful institutional and library support. Johnson County Community College granted me a sabbatical; the Beinecke Library at Yale University was very generous in granting me a research fellowship, and its librarians were second to none in assisting me. I also thank the librarians and staff at the Schomburg Center for Research in Black Culture in New York, the Amistad Library at Tulane University, the W. E. B. Du Bois Institute at Harvard University, and the Kansas Historical Society. Their financial and intellectual support and encouragement made this research an exciting and fulfilling adventure. This project could not have happened without the support of Harold Ober & Associates and the Hughes estate. Their permissions to publish the letters and photographs allowed this project to exist.

My deepest gratitude goes to my partner, Dr. John Edgar Tidwell. He supported my vision, encouraged my work and contributed to this book in very meaningful ways. My personal happiness and professional achievement with *My Dear Boy* are largely due to him.

I, John Edgar Tidwell, wish to acknowledge a number of people who were instrumental in bringing this project to fruition. To coeditor Dr. Carmaletta M. Williams I express my deepest gratitude for the invitation to participate in this incredible journey. Hughes scholarship, it seems, has greatly benefited from our foray into this famous author's mother and into his life and work as well. To make me a companion in this venture was an extremely generous act. When I was presented with a serious challenge to my physical well-being, Dr. Jon Heeb stepped in and provided me the reassuring care that restored me to a reasonable portion of good health. For his patient, sensitive medical treatment, I am immensely grateful.

For me, the largest inspiration for this book was provided by my mother and my son. On March 3, 2012, sometime after midnight, time stood still for a moment. In that instant, Mrs. Verlean L. Tidwell, my mother, made her transition from this world into the afterlife. Just a month short of her ninety-fifth birthday, she left quietly, quickly, but still all too soon. My personal goal was to present her with a book prominently displaying her name on the dedications page. It was to be a tribute, a clear statement acknowledging my most heartfelt appreciation for her constant stream of prayers, encouragement, and love. I hope that as she looks down from on high she is smiling with pride at what her son attempted to do in her name. I also dedicate my work on this book to my son, Levert Tidwell. As Langston Hughes wrote, life is indeed no crystal stair. It is filled with tacks and other impediments to life. My hope and prayer are that he will find in the example of his grandmother the strength to persist, the ability to be determined, and the sheer toughness to triumph over the pitfalls that beset us.

WORKS CONSULTED

Bernard, Emily, ed. *Remember Me to Harlem: The Letters of Langston Hughes and Carl Van Vechten*. New York: Vintage Books, 2001. Cited as CVV.

Berry, Faith, ed. *Good Morning Revolution: Uncollected Social Protest Writings*. New York: Lawrence Hill, 1973.

————. *Langston Hughes: Before and Beyond Harlem*. Westport: Lawrence Hill, 1983.

Bowen, Murray. *Family Therapy in Clinical Practice*. New York: Aronson, 1978.

Bump, Jerome. "The Family Dynamics of the Reception of Art." *Style* 31.2 (Summer 1997): 328–51.

Cohen, Paula Marantz. *The Daughter's Dilemma: Family Process and the Nineteenth-Century Domestic Novel*. Ann Arbor: University of Michigan Press, 1991.

De Santis, Christopher C., ed. *Langston Hughes and the Chicago Defender: Essays on Race, Politics, and Culture, 1942–1962*. Urbana: University of Illinois Press, 1995.

Dickinson, Donald C. *A Bio-Bibliography of Langston Hughes, 1902–1967*. Hamden, Conn.: Archon Press, 1972.

Fraser, Barbara, Linda McKay, and Lu Pease. "Interview with Michael Kerr." *Australian and New Zealand Journal of Family Therapy* 31.1 (2010): 100–109.

Gates, Henry Louis, Jr., and K. A. Appiah, eds. *Langston Hughes: Critical Perspectives Past and Present*. New York: Amistad, 1993.

Gill, C. M. "Martyring Veda: *Mildred Pierce* and Family Systems Theory." *Style* 44.1–2 (Spring/Summer 2010): 81–98.

Hallwas, John E. Introduction. *Spoon River Anthology.* By Edgar Lee Masters. Urbana: University of Illinois Press, 1992. 1–79.

Harper, Donna Akiba Sullivan. *Not So Simple: The "Simple" Stories by Langston Hughes.* Columbia: University of Missouri Press, 1995.

Harris, Susan K. *The Cultural Work of the Late Nineteenth-Century Hostess.* New York: Palgrave Macmillan, 2002.

Higginbotham, Evelyn Brooks. *Righteous Discontent: The Women's Movement in the Black Baptist Church, 1880–1920.* Cambridge: Harvard University Press, 1993.

Hill, Shirley Ann. *African American Children: Socialization and Development in Families.* Thousand Oaks, Calif.: Sage Publications, 1999.

Huggins, Nathan Irving. *Harlem Renaissance.* New York: Oxford University Press, 1971.

Hughes, Langston. *The Best of Simple.* 1961. New York: Farrar, Straus, Giroux, 1985.

———. *The Big Sea: An Autobiography.* 1940. New York: Hill and Wang, 1963.

———. *Five Plays by Langston Hughes.* Ed. Webster Smalley. Bloomington: Indiana University Press, 1968.

———. *Good Morning Revolution: Uncollected Writings of Langston Hughes.* Ed. Faith Berry. New York: Lawrence Hill, 1973.

———. *I Wonder as I Wander: An Autobiographical Journey.* 1956. New York: Hill and Wang, 1993. Cited as WW.

———. *The Negro Mother, and Other Dramatic Recitations.* New York: Golden Stair Press, 1931.

———. *Not without Laughter.* 1930. New York: Scribner Paperback, 1995.

———. "Simple and Me." 1945. *The Collected Works of Langston Hughes, Volume 9: Essays on Art, Race, Politics, and World Affairs.* Ed. Christopher C. De Santis. Columbia: University of Missouri Press, 2002. 257–62.

———. "To Maxim Lieber." 30 December 1935. *The Life of Langston Hughes,* vol. 1. By Arnold Rampersad. New York: Oxford University Press, 1986. 319.

———. "To Ulysses Kay." 31 May 1954. *Collected Works of Langston Hughes, Volume 5: The Plays to 1942.* Columbia: University of Missouri Press, 2002. 266.

Hughes, Langston, and Zora Neale Hurston. *Mulebone: A Comedy of Negro Life.* Ed. George Houston Bass and Henry Louis Gates Jr. New York: HarperPerennial, 1991.

Isaacs, Edith J. R. "The Negro in American Theater." *Theater Arts* 26.12 (1942): 494–543.

Jemie, Onwuchekwa. *Langston Hughes: An Introduction to the Poetry*. New York: Columbia University Press, 1976.

Johnson, Patrick, Walter Buboltz, and Eric Seemann. "Ego Identity Status: A Step in the Differentiation Process." *Journal of Counseling and Development* 81.2 (2003): 191–95.

Kennedy, David M. *Freedom from Fear: The American People in Depression and War, 1929–1945*. New York: Oxford University Press, 1999.

Knapp, John V. "Family Systems Psychotherapy, Literary Character, and Literature: An Introduction." *Style*, 31.2 (Summer 1997): 223–54.

Lang, Clarence. *Grassroots at the Gateway: Class Politics and Black Freedom Struggle in St. Louis, 1936–75*. Ann Arbor: University of Michigan Press, 2009.

Lewis, David Levering. *When Harlem Was in Vogue*. New York: Knopf, 1981.

Lowe, Walter. "Detriangulation of Absent Fathers in Single-Parent Black Families: Techniques of Imagery." *American Journal of Family Therapy* 28.1 (January 2000): 29–40.

Miller, R. Baxter. *The Art and Imagination of Langston Hughes*. Lexington: University Press of Kentucky, 1989.

Miller, Richard B., Shayne Anderson, and Davelyne Kaulana Keala. "Is Bowen Theory Valid: A Review of Basic Research." *Journal of Marital and Family Therapy*, 30.4 (October 2004): 453–66.

Moody, Joycelyn. *Sentimental Confessions: Spiritual Narratives of Nineteenth-Century African American Women*. Athens: University of Georgia Press, 2001.

Morrison, Toni. *Song of Solomon*. 1977. New York: Plume/Penguin Books, 1987.

Mullen, Edward J., ed. *Critical Essays on Langston Hughes*. Boston: GK Hall, 1986.

Nichols, Charles H., ed. *Arna Bontemps–Langston Hughes Letters, 1925–1967*. New York: Dodd, Mead, 1980.

O'Daniel, Therman B., ed. *Langston Hughes, Black Genius: A Critical Evaluation*. New York: William Morrow, 1971.

Rampersad, Arnold. "Biography and Afro-American Culture." *Afro-American Literary Study in the 1990s*. Ed. Houston Baker Jr. and Patricia Redmond. Chicago: University of Chicago Press, 1989. 194–208.

———. *The Life of Langston Hughes, Volume I: 1902–1941, I, Too, Sing America*. New York: Oxford University Press, 1986. Cited as ARI.

———. *The Life of Langston Hughes, Volume II: 1941–1967, I Dream a World*. New York: Oxford University Press, 1988. Cited as ARII.

Rootes, Katie M. Heiden, Peter J. Jankowski, and Steven J. Sandage. "Bowen Family Systems Theory and Spirituality: Exploring the Relationship between

Triangulation and Religious Questing." *Contemporary Family Therapy* 32 (2010): 89–101.

Sanders, Leslie. Introduction. *The Collected Works of Langston Hughes, Volume 5: The Plays to 1942.* Columbia: University of Missouri Press, 2002. 1–13.

Schiff, Sarah Eden. "Family Systems Theory as Literary Analysis: The Case of Philip Roth." *Philip Roth Studies,* 2.1 (Spring 2006): 25–46.

Skowron, Elizabeth A. "Differentiation of Self, Personal Adjustment, Problem Solving, and Ethnic Group Belonging among Persons of Color." *Journal of Counseling and Development,* 82.4 (Fall 2004): 447–56.

Smalley, Webster. Introduction. *Five Plays by Langston Hughes.* Bloomington: Indiana University Press, 1968. vii–xvii.

Storhoff, Gary. "'Anaconda Love': Parental Enmeshment in Toni Morrison's *Song of Solomon.*" *Style* 31.2 (Summer 1997): 290–309.

Tidwell, John Edgar. Introduction. *Black Moods: Collected Poems.* By Frank Marshall Davis. Urbana: University of Illinois Press, 2002. xxi–lxv.

———. Introduction. *Livin' the Blues.* By Frank Marshall Davis. Madison: University of Wisconsin Press, 1992. xiii–xxvii.

———. "The Sounds of Silence: Langston Hughes as a 'Down Low' Brother?" *Montage of a Dream: The Art and Life of Langston Hughes.* Ed. John Edgar Tidwell and Cheryl R. Ragar. Columbia: University of Missouri Press, 2007. 55–67.

———. "Two Writers Sharing: Sterling A. Brown, Robert Frost, and 'In Dives' Dive.'" *African American Review* 31.3 (1997): 399–408.

Tracy, Steven C. *Langston Hughes and the Blues.* Urbana: University of Illinois Press, 1988.

Watson, James G. *Thinking of Home: William Faulkner's Letters to His Mother and Father, 1918–1925.* New York: W. W. Norton, 1992.

———. *William Faulkner: Letters and Fictions.* Austin: University of Texas Press, 1987.

Williams, Carmaletta M. *Langston Hughes in the Classroom: Do Nothin' Till You Hear from Me.* Urbana: National Council of Teachers of English, 2006.

———. *"Only the Devils Danced."* PhD diss. University of Kansas, 2001.

Williams, Regennia N., and Carmaletta M. Williams. "Mother to Son: The Letters from Carrie Hughes Clark to Langston Hughes, 1928–1938." *Montage of a Dream: The Art and Life of Langston Hughes.* Ed. John Edgar Tidwell and Cheryl R. Ragar. Columbia: University of Missouri Press, 2007. 106–24.

INDEX

affect, 10, 15–16. *See also* Bowen,
　Murray
Amele. *See* McNaughton, Amelia
Amelie. *See* McNaughton, Amelia
American Mercury, 70, 74n1
anaconda love, 19
Annjee (fictional character), 166–68,
　170–71
appropriate fusion, 11, 174. *See also*
　Bowen, Murray
Aunt Hagar (fictional character),
　166–67, 169–70
Auntie Reed. *See* Campbell, Mary
　Reed

Baltimore Afro-American, 130, 132,
　156
Bernard, Emily, xvii, xix, 184
Berry, Faith, 4, 6
Bethune, Mary McLeod, 118, 120,
　175–76, 184n5
Big Sea, The (Hughes), x, 19, 89n1,
　165, 185

Black and White (film), xxv, 59
Black Masonic Fraternity, 4
Bontemps, Arna, xxiv, 59, 182, 184;
　Popo and Fifina (with Hughes), 58
Bowen, Murray, 8–10, 14–18, 40, 92,
　165, 172, 180; affect, 10, 15–16; ap-
　propriate fusion, 11, 174; differen-
　tiation, 8–9, 176; enmeshment, 8,
　19–20, 40–41, 92, 181; functional
　kin, 10, 172, 182; fusion, 8, 10, 13,
　16, 23, 129, 172–74, 178, 180–81;
　inappropriate fusion, 10, 12, 15–16,
　19, 25, 41, 90, 130, 169, 174, 176–77,
　180–82, 186; individuation,
　9–12, 16, 41, 173–74, 181; self-
　differentiation, 8–11, 16, 92, 172;
　triangulation, 8, 16–17, 41; undif-
　ferentiated child, 164–65
Brown, John, xxi, 4–5, 46n2, 47
Brown, Dr. Stanley, 121–22n2, 123,
　130, 135, 143n1, 143–45
Bump, Jerome, 7
Burns, Effie, 48n1